A NATION FOR ALL

How the Catholic Vision
of the Common Good
Can Save America
from the
Politics of Division

Chris Korzen and Alexia Kelley

Foreword by Senator Robert P. Casey Jr.

JOSSEY-BASS
A Wiley Imprint
www.josseybass.com

Published by Jossey-Bass.
A Wiley Imprint
989 Market Street, San Francisco, CA 94103-1741—www.josseybass.com

Jossey-Bass books and products are available through most bookstores. To contact Jossey-Bass
directly call our Customer Care Department within the U.S. at 800-956-7739, outside the U.S.
at 317-572-3986, or fax 317-572-4002.

Jossey-Bass also publishes its books in a variety of electronic formats. Some content that appears
in print may not be available in electronic books.

Library of Congress Cataloging-in-Publication Data

Korzen, Chris., date.
A nation for all : how the Catholic vision of the common good can save
America from the politics of division / Chris Korzen and Alexia Kelley.—
1st ed. ; foreword by Senator Robert P. Casey Jr.
p. cm.
Includes bibliographical references and index.
ISBN 978-0-470-25862-0 (cloth)
1. Common good—Religious aspects—Catholic Church. 2. Christianity and
politics—Catholic Church. 3. Christianity and politics—United States.
4. Christian sociology—Catholic Church. 5. Christian sociology—United
States. 6. Catholic Church—Doctrines. 7. Catholic Church—United
States. I. Kelley, Alexia K., 1966- II. Title.
BX1793.K59 2008
261.70973—dc22

2008009373

Printed in the United States of America
FIRST EDITION
HB Printing   10 9 8 7 6 5 4 3 2 1

Contents

"He that seeks the good of the many, seeks in consequence his own good."

—*Saint Thomas Aquinas*

Foreword

Public officials have a special obligation to seek the common good and to focus on the weak and vulnerable. My understanding of the common good comes from my family and my faith. Anyone growing up in a family of eight children learns about the importance of the common good, whether they want to or not. But I was especially blessed to have parents who taught me about the common good not by talking about it, but by the way they lived their lives and raised our family.

My understanding of the common good also comes from my faith: faith in God, that all things will ultimately work to His greater good; and my faith in the ingenuity, compassion, and generosity of all Americans to give their time, talent, and treasure to make this country truly great.

Yet as we seek the common good, we face substantial challenges in today's world of increasingly polarized public discourse and politics. Despite the tireless efforts of many sincere public servants, our political process is dominated by rhetoric at the expense of honesty, and simplified sound bites at the expense of thoughtful discussion of complex issues. Ideological rigidity fused with partisan hostility makes collaboration and consensus impossible. We all lose in such a toxic environment. But our biggest loss is the truth. With the truth goes our power to discern and fashion genuine solutions to the serious problems we face in the world today—abortion, war, caring for the poor, health care for the uninsured, immigration, violence in our communities, global warming, and more. And without the ability to forge real solutions based on civil and honest explorations of problems, we cannot be servants for the vulnerable people who need us most.

There is no question that this is a critical challenge for our country—perhaps one of the greatest challenges we face as it stands in the way of real progress on any issue.

I recognize this challenge within the culture of my own calling, and I am deeply committed, like so many other public servants and citizens, to working for genuine change, for authentic dialogue and consensus-building. *A Nation for All* reminds us that across the United States, there is movement away from the politics of polarization and division and toward a unified vision of the common good. The founders of *Catholics in Alliance for the Common Good* and *Catholics United* have written a thoughtful and important book that asks each of us to examine the ways in which we respond to the call of the common good and how we commit ourselves to serving the needs and preserving the dignity of the most vulnerable among us.

The common good must first be based upon a solid foundation of justice. As Saint Augustine taught us, "Without justice, what are kingdoms but great bands of robbers?" Justice cannot abide 34 million people living in poverty and 9.4 million children without health care. Justice cannot ignore the suffering of millions of parents in this country who have to face the chilling realization that they might have to send their child to bed hungry or that they simply cannot afford the medical treatment their child needs. Justice demands our understanding that the hungry, the impoverished, the uninsured, and the millions of other needy fellow citizens are not statistics; they are our brothers and sisters.

The common good resonates deeply with people from all faiths and political persuasions. Its origins go back as far as Plato and Aristotle, as well as to the words of Jesus. Since the birth of our Republic, Americans, and particularly public officials, have grappled with the role of religion—and its call to the common good—in the public square. Thomas Jefferson, in his first inaugural address in 1801, issued a call for citizens to "unite in common efforts for the common good."

In his 1960 campaign for President, Senator John F. Kennedy addressed this issue from the Catholic perspective in his famous speech to Protestant ministers in Houston. It is not surprising that Kennedy believed—and was able to convince American voters—that a Catholic could adhere to our constitutional separation of church and state, yet espouse a compassionate philosophy of governing informed by his religion. Kennedy recognized the common roots of Catholic social teaching and the Enlightenment-based philosophy that guided the dawn of our democracy.

We must unite as a country, Democrats and Republicans, behind the understanding that the common good requires us to value life, to honor a consistent ethic of life. As a pro-life Democrat, I believe that life begins at conception and ends when we draw our last breath. And I believe that the role of government is to protect, enrich, and value life for everyone, at every moment, from beginning to end.

But life extends beyond the womb and, in my view, neither party has done enough when it comes to pre- and post-natal life issues. We cannot realistically expect to tackle the difficult question of abortion without embracing the "radical solidarity" with women facing pregnancy, a kind of solidarity that Pope John Paul II spoke of many years ago. That is why I introduced legislation that seeks common ground in supporting pregnant women; that offers pregnant women, who are so often alone and without help, genuine and authentic choices and support both during pregnancy *and* after their babies are born. We cannot claim to be pro-life at the same time we are cutting support for programs like Medicaid, Head Start, and the State Children's Health Insurance Program.

The common good is also about community. Aristotle issued a challenge that survives the centuries when he said, "the state is a community of equals." If we truly lived by that credo,

I believe some of the endlessly circular arguments that characterize the most challenging political questions we face would simply not stand. If we live in a "community of equals," then policy arguments about health care for all uninsured children, housing for the homeless, supporting pregnant women, reducing the number of abortions, ending hunger, eradicating poverty, caring for our environment, preventing violence and war, and providing tough yet compassionate solutions to the problem of immigration—would be resolved without the kind of rancor and invective that characterizes our public discourse. And perhaps more important, we would recognize that we cannot easily prioritize the needs of these vulnerable people—all are equally interdependent and critical to the life and well-being of the community. The "us versus them" arguments would fade away. We would finally realize—we *are* them.

I believe we can and we must reaffirm our pursuit of both common ground and the common good. A *Nation for All* is an important roadmap for this pursuit, offering prudent and faithful guidance for our decisions and actions along the way. As people of faith, we are reminded of the words of the hymn "We Are Called":

> *We are called to act with justice,*
> *we are called to love tenderly,*
> *we are called to serve one another,*
> *to walk humbly with God.*

To reach the destination called the common good, we must traverse the road of the common ground. It is not an easy journey. But it is a worthy one. And it is the only way in which we can truly create *a nation for all*.

Senator Robert P. Casey Jr.

March 14, 2008

Acknowledgments

This book was truly a labor of love, and it would not have been possible without the participation, contributions, and support of many of our colleagues, staff, donors, board members, and friends. We are continually renewed and invigorated by the conviction of those in the Catholic social justice movement who have devoted their lives to the Church's call to justice, human dignity, and the common good: men and women religious, lay leaders, young people, activists, academics, and bishops whose daily practice of the common good is already at work transcending the politics of division.

We are grateful to the staff of both of our organizations, including John Cosgriff, Krista Stevens, Brian Murray, Sarah Sweeney, and Brandon Griffith, who conducted research and checked facts and figures. John Gehring, senior writer at Catholics in Alliance, contributed significantly to Chapter One, "The Common Good," and provided valuable editing and review of other chapters. Pat Wheeler also reviewed the manuscript and offered important insights. James Salt provided much support and encouragement.

Several members of the academic community generously reviewed various chapters and provided important comments throughout the project: Professor Lisa Sowle Cahill of Boston College, Professor David O'Brien of Holy Cross College, Professor Vincent Miller of Georgetown University, Professor Jennifer Mason McAward of the Notre Dame Law School,

Professor John Sniegocki of Xavier University, Professor Kristin Heyer of Loyola Marymount University, and Reverend Thomas Reese, S.J., of Woodstock Theological Seminary. We are grateful to Reverend Kenneth Himes, O.F.M., of Boston College, editor of *Modern Catholic Social Teaching* (a resource that provided important guidance for this project), and to Reverend David Hollenbach, S.J., whose thinking and writing on the common good, in particular *The Common Good in Christian Ethics*, informed our efforts. We also express our thanks to Reverend Thomas Massaro, S.J., of the School of Theology and Ministry at Boston College for his inspirational work in the field of religion and public life.

The trustees and donors of Catholics in Alliance for the Common Good and Catholics United provide the stewardship and funding support that make projects like this book possible. We are grateful for their support and investment in our respective organizations.

We also want to acknowledge and thank the boards of directors of both of our organizations for providing leadership and support and for doing so much to advance the common good and the Catholic social tradition. In particular, Catholics in Alliance board member Frank Doyle, who offered excellent advice and comments on the entire manuscript; Catholics in Alliance cofounder Tom Perriello, whose vision and passion for the common good provided much inspiration for this book; and Ambassador Elizabeth Frawley Bagley, who provided leadership and support for our work from the beginning.

Sheryl Fullerton, Alison Knowles, and Joanne Clapp Fullagar at Jossey-Bass, as well as Gail Ross and Howard Yoon of the Gail Ross literary agency, helped us move this book from concept to reality. All are a joy to work with and provided essential expertise, support, and guidance.

Finally, we want to thank our dear families and friends for their support, patience, and encouragement. Without their generous understanding and enthusiasm, we would not be able to do this work.

Introduction

The United States continues to serve as a shining example of peace and democracy—a model to be admired and emulated by those who value freedom and human rights. The reasons are clear. Our Constitution guarantees profound political and economic liberties. We have built an American creed that promises that with hard work, anyone can be anything one wants to be. Many peoples of the world can only dream of such opportunity, as evidenced by the multitudes who risk everything for the chance of starting new lives here. Our economy has been the largest and most successful in all of human history, and we have one of the highest standards of living in the world. We are the source of much of the world's technological and industrial innovation and have built one of the greatest education systems in history.

Indeed, it is our commitment to democracy that sustains and defines us as a people. Democracy guarantees our right to life, liberty, and the pursuit of happiness, and despite all of our differences allows us to work together to achieve the dream of freedom. Democracy makes it possible for us to come from so many backgrounds—ethnically, religiously, racially, and politically—and still call ourselves Americans. The fact that the United States is the most diverse nation in the history of the world is a big enough deal. But the fact that it is the most diverse *and* the most prosperous is downright amazing. That we can claim both of these superlatives at once is not a coincidence. Our American democracy works because of the multitude of ideas and perspectives Americans bring to the political table, and because we have found ways to work together to realize our shared national goals.

However, the very idea of America is now threatened by a dangerous and insidious force—dangerous because it tears at the very unity that has sustained this country for more than two centuries, and insidious because it's a threat that comes not from foreign invaders but from within our own borders. This threat can go by many names. In this book, we call it the *politics of division*.

What is the politics of division? If you've ever watched political talking heads screaming at each other on a cable TV news program, if you've ever listened to our leaders resort to scare tactics and name-calling as ways to advance their own agendas, if you've ever seen an election campaign attack ad, then you've witnessed the politics of division firsthand. The politics of division takes place when our leaders encourage us to put aside our commonalities and focus on our differences. It reduces our political system to a popularity contest (the winners in the politics of division aren't necessarily the people with the best ideas; they are often the ones who fight the dirtiest) and a childish struggle that seems more appropriate to a playground than our public square. The few who benefit from the politics of division win money and power. The many who lose out are regarded as mere collateral damage in what the media have taken to calling the "culture war."

The politics of division is designed to distract us from the things that really matter. The United States of America is still the greatest nation this world has ever seen, but the signs increasingly suggest that we are losing our way. We read about this decline in the papers every day: war, poverty, climate change, lack of health care and retirement protections, a housing crisis, a host of economic problems that threaten to end the middle-class way of life as we know it. For the first time in American history, members of new generations are being told not to expect to do as well as their parents. In a nation that prides itself on freedom and opportunity for all, the gap between rich and poor continues to widen at an ever-increasing pace.

Those who engage in the politics of division present us with easy solutions that blame others for this downward spiral. "If we could just get rid of the immigrants and the liberals and the gays," they tell us, "everything will be OK." Others point fingers at all men for discrimination against women or blame the wealthy for all the problems of society. Some tell us the problem is that our taxes are too high and public spending is out of control. "Vote for us," they say, "and we will protect you from the all the bad people who are ruining your way of life, including the government."

It's not enough to blame others for the politics of division. Like it or not, we've all become a part of the problem. We've bought into a way of life that promises short-term solutions, easy answers, and instant gratification. In many ways, our biggest enemy is a culture of greed, materialism, and excessive individualism that has come to characterize our society and politics. The politics of division, which seeks to isolate us from one another, is only able to flourish in this go-it-alone culture.

Let's be clear. Self-reliance and self-expression are cherished American principles, and scientific, economic, and social progress would not be possible if our culture did not value individual achievement. When *Time* magazine named "you" its 2006 person of the year, for example, it did so not because more people were better off than at any other time in history but because the Internet provides unprecedented opportunities for average people to make themselves known in the wider world. But the excesses of this go-it-alone culture are hard to avoid, and they saturate nearly every aspect of American life. From the moment we are born, Americans are bombarded with TV, movies, and advertising that tell us that the highest virtue is to think about ourselves first. Success means having the biggest house, the largest car, and the latest technological gadgets. In modern-day American society, our worth is measured not by the size of our hearts or the quality of our character but by the money we make, the possessions we acquire, and the size of our investment portfolios.

In the past, our leaders in Washington would seldom hesitate to call on Americans to sacrifice and to work together to accomplish a greater good. Facing the very real threat of communism in January 1961, President John F. Kennedy famously called on Americans to "ask not what your country can do for you" but rather to "ask what you can do for your country." But after the terrorist attacks of September 11, 2001, President George W. Bush asked us to go shopping. He would take care of Osama bin Laden. In exchange, he asked only for our "continued participation and confidence in the American economy." In effect, he said, the best thing we could do for our country was to buy more stuff.

Perhaps the biggest reason that our go-it-alone culture persists is that it follows a basic plausible logic: if everyone just looks after oneself, everyone will be looked after. But there's a fatal flaw in this thinking. Human beings by nature are social creatures. We're hard-wired to build communities and work together, and none of us is capable of reaching our full potential as individuals without the help and participation of others. Without doctors and nurses, health care would be primitive at best. Without farmers, every one of us would spend the majority of our time searching for food or growing it ourselves. Without teachers, there would be little primary education, let alone high schools and universities. Someone has to build the cars and planes and computers that keep modern society moving along. People need people. There's just no getting around it.

Self-reliance is an important and essential value in America. But so is building strong and nurturing communities. There was a time in the not-too-distant past when Americans believed we should look out for one another, when our elected officials saw to it that public policy reflected this value, and when we knew how to balance the value of self-reliance with a strong concern for the larger community. Faced with an economic depression of unparalleled proportions, in 1933 President Franklin D. Roosevelt instituted the New Deal—a set of sweeping reforms that used public funds to provide jobs and direct assistance to millions of impoverished Americans—effectively ensuring that all would shoulder the burden of recovery. In the 1950s, President Dwight D. Eisenhower worked to implement a major expansion of Social Security, expanding its benefits to some ten million more Americans. Kennedy reminded us during his famous inaugural address that "if a free society cannot help the many who are poor, it cannot save the few who are rich."

Somewhere along the way, we decided we'd be better off as a people if we all stopped caring about each other and just looked out for ourselves. But the sad irony of this approach is just how much it is hurting us as individuals. How many Americans are now working fifty-, sixty-, even eighty-hour weeks just to try to maintain their modest ways of life? How many are forced to commute three, four, five, or more hours a day for lack of affordable housing near their jobs or because quiet neighborhoods and good schools are being pushed farther and farther from the cities?

What about health care? The United States is the only industrialized nation in the world without full health coverage for all its citizens, even though we spend more on health care than any other country. We're told that this is a good thing, that it provides consumers choice in the marketplace. But who really benefits when some forty-seven million Americans are uninsured and when the costs of health insurance are weighing down millions more families and placing a heavy burden on U.S. businesses?

The effect of this go-it-alone culture on the American family is catastrophic. Children without adequate health coverage; parents who spend so much time working that they don't have time left over to spend with their kids; children who are raised by television, learning the values of consumer society instead of the values of family and community; children exposed to sex and violence when they are far too young.

Many of those who participate in the politics of division want us to believe that gay people or immigrants are the biggest threat to the American family. But studies show that the number one thing that couples fight over is money. Our fast-paced consumer lifestyle, the disposable society (which teaches us that everything can be thrown away when it has outgrown its usefulness to us—even our marriages), the constant threat of job loss, and the lack of retirement protections—these are dire threats to the family. And they are more damaging and insidious than any we have ever seen.

We're told that the best way to end poverty is for the poor to stop being so lazy and get to work. But how can they do this when the deck is so firmly stacked against them? Inner-city school districts are chronically underfunded, and rising housing costs make it hard enough to pay the rent, let alone realize the dream of owning a home. New generations learn to lower their own expectations of success, creating a cycle of poverty with catastrophic effects. Poverty feeds crime and drug abuse. Research consistently shows that a majority of women who seek abortions do so for economic reasons. Globally, poverty and wealth inequality often breed war and armed conflict and force millions to leave their homelands and immigrate, often illegally, to nations like the United States. The vast disparities between the wealth of a few in our country and the poverty of so many in the rest of the world allow terrorist leaders to feed off hopelessness and instability and recruit new blood at an unprecedented rate.

And then there is the question of resources, which is closely connected to the health of our natural environment and our national security. For decades now, America has been living like there is no tomorrow. Gas-guzzling cars, uncontrolled development, too much trash. The United States, as studies show, uses between a quarter and a third of the world's resources even though it contains only 5 percent of the world's population. All this has come at extraordinary cost. Scientists almost universally agree that human activity is a primary cause of global climate change.

Our go-it-alone culture has spun off a number of cure-all solutions that claim to help improve the lives of Americans while diminishing our responsibility to build a society in which everyone can benefit. "Trickle-down economics" argued that we could best benefit society by providing the biggest tax breaks for the wealthiest Americans, whose surplus income would translate into increased employment opportunities for the working and middle classes. The "thousand points of light" doctrine held that social progress was the province of private enterprise only, not of the state. More recently, "compassionate conservatism" tried to shift more of the responsibility for caring for society's neediest away from the government and toward private institutions. These ideas have two things in common: they demonize both government and taxes as "burdensome" to the American people, and they simply do not work.

While we were writing this book, Chris was often reminded of a cartoon he keeps in his office, a one-panel *Peanuts* spoof that shows Lucy holding a football in front of an uneasy-looking Charlie Brown. "If you cut taxes on the rich," Lucy is saying, "they'll invest that money and create jobs for everyone." What comes next—the image of Charlie Brown flying helplessly through the air after a snickering Lucy has pulled the ball away at the last minute—is left to our imagination. But the point is clear: as well intentioned as an idea like compassionate conservatism may be, it is in fact neither compassionate nor conservative, having done little more than accelerate the divide between rich and poor and create budget deficits that threaten the entire economy. Even as we write these words, social observers are warning of the eventual demise of the middle class.

Does this mean that we should give people a free ride and expect the government to take care of those who are capable of improving their own situation? Absolutely not. What we're saying is that it's incumbent on *all* of us—and even in our own interest—to make sure that each and every American has the opportunity to be all that he or she can be. The choice between self-reliance and community responsibility is a false one. We need both. When hunger, lack of education, inadequate health care, or the absence of parents to instill good values prevents a child from realizing his or her dreams, we all suffer. And we fall far short of our responsibility to care for one another and of our American potential.

Why This Book?

We decided to write this book because we believe it's time to put an end to both the politics of division and the culture of going it alone. They both hurt us individually and as a nation. It's often said that the duty of each generation is to leave the world a better place for the next. For the sake of our children, our grandchildren, and the entire world, we need either to change course or risk the extinction of our democratic way of life. We need to work together to build a nation for all.

But we also decided to write this book because we believe that we have a solution to the politics of division—or at least know of an answer. That answer is the *common good*. What is the common good? On its most basic level, the common good means building a society that benefits all the people in it. But it is also important to emphasize what the common good is not. President Bush, for instance, cited the common good as a justification for his wiretapping program, and some big oil companies have used the common good as a marketing slogan for products that harm the environment. Certain socialist philosophies assert that the common good means doing the most good for the most people—but this can have the effect of reducing people to mere instruments of society, especially those who aren't part of the "most."

As a philosophical idea, the common good finds deep roots in the Roman Catholic tradition, which recognizes every human life as a sacred image of God and holds that it is our social duty to ensure that *each and every* person has the opportunity to reach his or her full potential. At the core of the Catholic vision of the common good is the principle that we are social beings; our lives are intricately interrelated. In the words of Pope John Paul II, "Our human interdependence . . . is not a feeling of vague compassion or shallow distress at the misfortunes of so many people, both near and far. On the contrary, it is a firm and persevering determination to commit oneself to the common good; that is to say to the good of all and of each individual, because we are all really responsible for all."

We look out for our neighbors because of love and the understanding that we are all safer, healthier, and freer in a world where we take care of one another. A culture of the common good demands justice for all Americans and for citizens of other nations. It is based on a belief that the health, security, and prosperity of America goes hand in hand with the well-being of all peoples and that our common humanity is stronger than our divisions.

We are, in a moral and strategic sense, in this together. As people of faith, we must overcome a culture of excessive materialism and individualism and recognize our duty to the human community as an essential part of responsible citizenship. This is not solely a Catholic value—when the preamble to the U.S. Constitution begins by invoking "We the people" and speaks of our need to "promote the general Welfare," it serves as a reminder that concern for the common good is also a founding principle of our nation.

It's true that this is in large part a book for and by members of the Catholic Church. But adherents of many other faiths (indeed, even those who don't subscribe to organized religion at all) will find much to take away from these pages. The Catholic vision of the common good is grounded first and foremost in the universal ideas that we're all created equal, that our purpose in this world is to love and care for one another, and that we're better off as individuals when we work together. As theological as this concept may seem, you don't need an advanced degree or any particular religious instruction to understand it. Human beings are born with an innate ability to recognize our essential connections to one another. The common good isn't just a philosophical idea. It's something that makes a whole lot of sense.

A third reason for writing this book stems from the increasing prevalence of religious values in the American civic debate. We, the authors of this book, have devoted our lives to working at the intersection of faith and politics, and so we feel strongly that the values of faith can play a vital role in our public policy by focusing on the goals of greater justice for all and the common good. But we also understand that in recent years—perhaps more often than not—some of those seeking power have misused faith for their own political gain. In the spirit of the politics of division, they have used faith to drive wedges between voters and even to advance policies that work against the common good. Where religion and politics are concerned, it's time to set the record straight.

Finally, we want to make it abundantly clear that while we do put forth in this book a sometimes harsh critique of the current direction of our nation's politics and culture, we do not intend to pick on any particular political parties, candidates, or leaders. Our goal, rather, is to take a closer look at the policies and ideas that hold sway in this era of the politics of division and to offer a vision of the common good that can benefit all human beings. We believe that both major political parties have in recent years failed to live up to the call to the common good and sincerely hope that all our leaders can learn from the recent past and work together to forge a positive new path for the future.

Recovering Faith

The years following the 2004 presidential election witnessed a tremendous upsurge of interest in faith and politics. Scores of books on the subject hit the shelves, and commentators discussed church and state on the TV talk shows and in the editorial pages. It seemed that all at once, religion was the most interesting, frightening, or exciting new theme in politics (depending on your perspective). Everyone wanted to know what this meant for the future of our democracy.

What accounts for this perception? Well, for one thing, something *had* in fact changed. Faith and religious values played a more important role in the 2004 election than perhaps any other in history—so much so that many pundits credited the election's outcome to the turnout of a political demographic called "values voters." Values voters were those of us whose political engagement was inspired by deeply held—often religious—convictions. And according to conventional wisdom, President Bush's reelection campaign succeeded by putting unprecedented resources into courting values voters, a strategy that bore fruit in swing states like Ohio.

But as it turns out, many values voters didn't completely agree with the president's particular take on the concept of "moral values." While conventional wisdom—as framed by President Bush's campaign—held that values voters were concerned primarily with issues of abortion and same-sex marriage, a post-election Zogby poll cosponsored by the Catholic social justice group Pax Christi USA showed that common good issues like poverty, greed, and materialism actually held enormous sway in the election. This didn't mean that values voters didn't care about all the other vital and urgent moral concerns. It just meant that many voters understood that we needed to address the cultural, economic, and social causes of our problems—including our moral problems—as well as their symptoms. Catholics are among the most highly educated members of our society. We head major corporations, operate some of the most prestigious colleges and universities in the world, and occupy five of nine seats on the U.S. Supreme Court. Yet in 2004, the media and political culture warriors told us that when it came to politics, we shouldn't try to think for ourselves. Instead they told us that voting Catholic was nothing more than a simple formula. It didn't matter at all which candidate we judged would do more to protect human life or save the ailing institution of marriage. All that was supposed to matter to us was which candidate *said* he or she cared the most about these issues.

One need look no further than the practical effects of this politics of division to see what an absolute disaster this kind of thinking was. In the wake of the 2004 election, the Iraq War—supported by members of both major political parties—morphed from an ill-advised folly into a complete humanitarian catastrophe. Civil liberties were curtailed, and torture scandals came to light. Hurricane Katrina turned the Gulf Coast into its own kind of war zone—proving once and for all our government's near-complete lack of effective concern for the poor and disenfranchised.

Few people were left unaffected. As taxes were cut on the wealthiest Americans, more ordinary people went without health insurance, the economy sputtered, jobs went overseas, and the global climate crisis came into sharper focus. For all the talk about protecting the unborn, little progress was made on ending abortion. For all the promises to protect the family, hardworking American families faced an increasingly bleak future.

What do these issues have to do with Catholic teaching? Everything. For Catholics, the untold story of the 2004 election was that the Church's social teachings encompass a broad and deep array of moral concerns and, above all else, that they encourage us to see how each issue is connected to others. The Catholic tradition envisions a society in which we care for each other and promote the common good for all. In this vision, there is no permanent home for greed, materialism, or a go-it-alone culture that makes a mockery of human life and dignity. To underscore this point, in 2003 the United States Conference of Catholic Bishops (USCCB) released a document called *Faithful Citizenship: A Catholic Call to Political Responsibility*, which listed some fifty issues relevant in the 2004 election—everything from war to poverty to abortion to climate change and the death penalty. And more important than any one of these issues was the overriding moral concern to protect the life and dignity of all human beings and ensure that our society benefits everyone, especially the poor.

In short, the bishops said, it's all about the common good.

A New Movement for the Common Good

The path that led us to write this book began in the spring of 2004. Chris was a theology graduate student in Boston, and Alexia was working for a nonprofit environmental firm in Washington, D.C. Neither of us was involved in politics or had ever met, and both of us were very happy in our respective positions. But all this was about to change as we became increasingly aware of the poor representation of Catholic values in the election and the deliberate attempt by some partisan operatives to suppress authentic Church teaching on the common good.

One day in May, Chris got a call from his friend James Salt, an activist who was working for a Catholic social justice organization in Washington. James and some other Catholic friends wanted to do something to promote the USCCB's *Faithful Citizenship* document, and they had come up with the idea of building an online voting guide to compare George Bush and John Kerry on the important Catholic values and political issues outlined in the document. They spent the summer researching the campaigns' positions and building the Web site. On August 30, 2004, they launched the guide under the name "Catholic Voting Project."

The Catholic Voting Project was really just a handful of young Catholics with no offices and no budget. Many of its "staff" had never even met face to face, their only contact being through e-mail and conference calls. For his part, Chris became the group's spokesperson merely because as a student, he was the only one who was unencumbered by a full-time job. In total, the project spent less than $500 during the entire campaign.

And yet it was an immediate and unprecedented success. Media outlets like the Associated Press and many regional newspapers picked up on the story, and Catholics across the country who were yearning for a message more consistent with their faith found that the project provided a much-needed breath of fresh air. From all corners of our nation, Catholics wrote to thank us for providing a faithful alternative to the far right's Catholic voting formula.

Meanwhile, Alexia had been working for two years in the field of renewable energy, having spent the previous decade at the Catholic Campaign for Human Development, the U.S. Catholic Church's antipoverty initiative. Like Chris, she was intent on staying out of partisan politics. But reading the newspapers in the spring of 2004, with her father serving in Iraq, she was increasingly worried that the Catholic vision of peace, social justice, and the common good was sorely missing from the 2004 election debates. Concerned about the threats to human life and peace posed by the Iraq War, she began to be convinced that John Kerry was more committed to a responsible withdrawal than his opponent.

In October 2004, the Democratic National Committee offered Alexia a consulting position for the last four weeks of the campaign. It was a difficult decision, because like Chris, she had been intent on staying out of partisan politics and was enjoying her new field of work. In the end, Alexia decided to take a leave from her job. She felt that the Democratic Party needed help understanding the concerns of Catholic voters, as well as the vision of the common good and respect for human dignity at the heart of our faith. Perhaps she could help rebuild this relationship that had historically done much to advance the call to peace and the common good in our country.

What concerned us most about the suppression of authentic Catholic values in 2004 was as much *what* happened as *why* it happened. We were told that a silent but strong majority had slowly been building to challenge the excesses of modern society and return our nation to authentic conservative values, which included a stated commitment to faith and family. But in reality, these appealing values were a smokescreen for a secular conservative political agenda of minimal government, an option for the wealthy, reckless foreign policy, and a rejection of the public good—all of which flew in the face of the Catholic tradition.

Although the president managed to present his candidacy as the one that best embodied authentic Christian values, many Americans felt that it really missed the mark when it came to advancing concern for the common good, both as a core principle of our Christian faith and as a crucial value at stake in the election. For the most part, the movement that supposedly reelected the president had not nearly as many members as the pundits claimed, a misperception perpetuated by an advanced organizing operation and millions of dollars of political cash. The great lesson of 2004 was that the religious far right owed its dominance to its superior ability to deliver its message, not to the theological accuracy of that message. Determined to ensure that this could never happen again, we sat down with other leaders in the Catholic social justice movement in 2005 to determine the best way to restore the values at the heart of our faith to the national dialogue on faith and politics. Catholics in Alliance for the Common Good and Catholics United were born.

Catholics in Alliance (http://www.catholicsinalliance.org), the organization Alexia directs, has a primary mission of providing communications and grassroots organizing support to organizations within the Catholic social justice movement. These organizations—Catholic peace and justice groups, grassroots organizations, and men's and women's religious orders—have worked for decades to communicate the values at the heart of our faith but were having an increasingly difficult time doing so in the face of the rapid news cycles and highly sophisticated media campaigns. In 2006, Catholics in Alliance also released a nonpartisan "common good" voter guide to promote the Catholic social tradition and initiated a grassroots outreach program to help Catholics act locally to promote an authentic vision of the common good.

Chris's organization, Catholics United (http://www.catholics-united.org), has built a new kind of grassroots presence in the Catholic community, using the Internet to mobilize Catholics who traditionally have not considered themselves activists, and tackling some important legislative initiatives that bear on the common good. In 2007, it worked to advance policy to bring the Iraq War to a responsible end and to expand heath care coverage for uninsured children, going so far as to challenge a number of members of Congress who had voted against the latter legislation. It also supported congressional efforts to find common ground solutions to the abortion debate, authoring a study that showed that providing family and social supports was the best way to reduce abortions.

Together, with the tireless effort of the Catholic social justice movement, our many affiliated organizations, and the broader Christian and interfaith social justice movements, we have managed to turn the national dialogue on faith and politics around in just a few short years. The culture warriors of the religious far right no longer enjoy a stranglehold on faithful political engagement. In fact, their influence has declined significantly as a new generation of conservative leaders has come to embrace ending poverty, addressing the root causes of abortion, and protecting the environment as core Christian ideals. Many of these leaders have stopped blaming scapegoats such as gay people and immigrants for the problems of society and have been more willing to look to our shared responsibility in perpetuating the cultural excesses of greed and materialism.

We have helped educate the media to understand the values voter as a dynamic freethinker, not a single-issue robot, who sees a unifying value in the common good and the need to refocus our national concern on the deeper cultural threats to society: poverty, the devaluing of human life and dignity, loss of community, rampant materialism, and a go-it alone culture.

Most important, in parishes and small faith groups across the country, Catholics who have felt voiceless are now finding that they have a right and a duty to make themselves heard. From the environment and the crisis in Darfur to the war in Iraq and building the essential conditions for a culture of life, everyday Catholics are now taking on a host of crucial political and social concerns.

Finding Solutions

This book is not intended as a laundry list of all the troubles facing our nation and our world. Although we have posed the problem of the politics of division in this Introduction, we hope readers will perceive the book as a presentation of *solutions*—based on our own ideas, the traditions of our church, and the thoughts of our community on how to realize the Christian and American dreams of building a society in which all of us have the opportunity to reach our full human potential.

In Chapter One, "The Common Good," we explore the philosophical and theological ideas behind the common good and delve into its significance and relevance in modern-day America. We take a deeper look at Catholic social and political thought in Chapter Two, "The Catholic Social Tradition." Based on scripture and centuries of Christian teaching, the Catholic social tradition addresses the social, economic, and cultural problems of modern society. It is made up primarily of papal documents that connect the spiritual and social missions of the Church and make clear our faith's commitment to the common good.

Chapter Three, "Church and State," examines the rightful distinctions between religion and politics in both the American and Catholic traditions. In it, we address directly the question of how people of faith can express their religious values in the public square without violating the Bill of Rights and the American belief in freedom of religion.

In Chapter Four, "Voting Catholic," we look specifically at the duties and responsibilities of the Catholic voter and tackle some unresolved controversies that arose during the 2004 election. Can Catholics vote in good conscience for candidates with the "wrong" positions on certain issues? Here we address this and other pressing questions. Chapter Five, "An Agenda for the Common Good," expands this thinking and offers a relevant and timely vision for public policy that advances the common good.

We conclude our book with Chapter Six, "Practicing the Common Good," which looks at ways we can build the common good in all areas of society—through our politics, economics, and culture, and in our individual lives. We offer some real choices to make in these areas in order to overcome the false choices of the politics of division. And we take a look at the future of faith and politics in America, including the role the media play in communicating the values of Catholic and other faith communities.

The Common Good

In recent years, references to the common good have papered the public square. Presidential and congressional candidates infuse their stump speeches with common good language. Political think tanks organize forums on the common good. It's debated in the pages of intellectual journals and the mainstream media. Senator Robert Casey Jr. of Pennsylvania, for example, made the common good the defining theme of his successful 2006 campaign against incumbent Republican Senator Rick Santorum, who had written his own book about conservatism and the common good.

It's not hard to see why this often misunderstood concept of moral and political philosophy has caught on with a new generation of public officials, political consultants, and grassroots social justice activists. At a time when war, corporate scandals, the fraying of traditional community bonds, and the economic dislocations of globalization have left many people feeling adrift in a rapidly changing world, Americans are hungry for a new vision of leadership and community. We recognize the potential for something bigger and better than narrow partisan agendas, divides between so-called red and blue states, and pandering politicians whose most urgent priorities seem to be promising earmarks, tax cuts, or whatever else tests well in the polls. We're looking for leaders who aren't afraid to challenge us to embrace a cause greater than ourselves.

In his book *Why Americans Hate Politics*, *Washington Post* columnist E. J. Dionne argues that many Americans have given up on politics because instead of real solutions to our most serious moral and political challenges, it presents a collection of false choices such as civil liberties *or* national security, economic growth *or* a healthy environment. These false choices obscure the fact that our success as individuals is closely tied to our collective well-being. A hallmark of the politics of division is the reduction of our public debates to either-or categories that inevitably paralyze our political process and impede progress toward actual solutions. Americans are tired of this stalemate and desperately want our values to move us forward as a united nation. A 2006 poll by the Center for American Progress asked Americans from across the political spectrum about the role of faith and values in public life. Sixty-eight percent strongly agreed that "our government should be committed to the common good." Seventy-one percent said that "Americans are becoming too materialistic."

Politics is more than a hodgepodge of policy proposals. It's about a larger story of who we are as people and what we aspire to as a society. Thomas Jefferson instilled the rhetorical seeds of revolution with the power of what in his day was a radical idea: the belief that all people are created equal and have rights and dignity that come from a creator, not a monarch. Reverend Martin Luther King Jr. challenged the conscience of a segregated nation to live up to the ideals of those principles. A century and a half after the end of the Civil War, we still pursue, in the language of Abraham Lincoln at Gettysburg, the "unfinished work" of freedom and justice for all.

Itself a close relative to the American ideal of a nation for all, the common good has helped influence some of our most important political and social movements. In this chapter, we will examine how we can reclaim the best of this tradition for our own historical moment when we face so many challenges that require us to recognize our common humanity and destiny. We will also explore how embracing a Catholic vision of the common good—one rooted in the essential dignity of the human person and the specific demands of justice—can help save this idea from becoming just another political slogan.

Origins of the Common Good

As a philosophical idea, the common good has roots in many sources: classical philosophy, the Catholic social tradition, our American experiment, and the wisdom of many faiths. In the fourth century B.C., Aristotle first articulated the notion that a just society must recognize the common good as ultimately "nobler and more divine" than individual desires. "The good is justice," he wrote, "in other words, the common interest." In the thirteenth century, Saint Thomas Aquinas developed Aristotle's concept of the common good and linked it closely to the Christian tradition. Framing the common good as a philosophical extension of the biblical prophets' call for justice and Christ's message to love our neighbors as ourselves, he emphasized that the common good is not a threat to our own personal interests; rather, our individual well-being is intricately connected to the health of the community. "He that seeks the good of many," Aquinas insisted, "seeks in consequence his own good."

The transformation of our nation from a fragmented colonial society under British imperial rule to an independent and unified republic put to test a bold democratic experiment that honored the "unalienable rights" of individuals. It also recognized the vital need for a responsive government "of the people, by the people, for the people" that represented the collective interests of citizens working together for shared goals of peace and prosperity. While this communitarian spirit has sometimes clashed with our nation's value of "rugged individualism," an authentic understanding of the common good reminds us that the fate of our neighbors here and around the world is closely connected to our own destiny. Especially in a time when globalization is making our world smaller, we can no longer afford to address in a vacuum such issues as war, abortion, climate change, and energy policy. For our own good and the good of others, we must as a society begin to make these essential connections.

The common good is a familiar concept for people of faith. Catholics and Protestants alike believe in the moral obligations of individuals and government to build a just society that responds to the needs of all its members, particularly the poor and most vulnerable. In the Jewish tradition, the Hebrew prophets denounced greed and hunger for power while reminding the community to care for the poor, the widows, and the suffering. Islam stresses the importance of community and the responsibility of government to serve the common good. Centuries of interfaith dialogue have been built on this shared commitment to justice for all God's children and respect for universal human dignity.

A Catholic Vision of the Common Good

Unlike the vague and simplistic references to the common good that often pervade our public debates today, the Catholic vision of the common good is as clear as it is challenging. The *Compendium of the Social Doctrine of the Church*, which the Vatican released in 2004, notes that the specific "demands" of the common good are deeply connected to the fundamental dignity and rights of the human person:

> These demands concern above all the commitment to peace, the organization of the State's powers, a sound juridical system, the protection of the environment, and the provision of essential services to all, some of which are at the same time human rights: food, housing, work, education and access to culture, transportation, basic health care, the freedom of communication and expression, and the protection of religious freedom.

A robust commitment to the common good dates to the very beginnings of our faith and is rooted in both the Old and New Testaments. The Hebrew scriptures call readers to look beyond their own self interest to create a just and healthy community; and the Gospels teach us to love God with all of our heart, mind, and soul, *and* to love our neighbors as ourselves.

The common good also requires a concern for the entire world community. In the sixteenth century, the earliest followers of Saint Ignatius of Loyola—the Jesuits—were among the first Westerners to travel beyond Europe, inspired by a global vision of the common good. In 1963, Pope John XXIII introduced the phrase "universal common good" in the Catholic social tradition in recognition of the duty to promote the good of our neighbors around the globe as well as at home. Later, Pope John Paul II spoke eloquently about a "globalization of solidarity" among people of the world committed to peace and justice. This vision of solidarity is an important counterpoint to profit-driven globalization, which can idolize the marketplace at the expense of human dignity.

While Catholic teaching values the importance of personal responsibility and respects the distinct spheres of church and state, it insists that government has a vital role to play in assuming duties that the market or individuals alone cannot or will not meet. The *Catechism of the Catholic Church* asserts that the common good is the very "reason the political authority exists," and other elements of Church teaching make clear that societies should not make an idol of the marketplace and that "ownership of goods be equally accessible to all." By promoting living wages, recognizing the value of labor unions, and affirming the dignity of work, the Catholic Church has offered a consistent moral critique of the sort of minimalist governing philosophy that abandons individuals to the vagaries of the marketplace or to the whims of charity.

There was a time when a Catholic vision of the common good helped inspire and shape seminal movements in American political history. Franklin Roosevelt drew heavily from Catholic social thought in his New Deal agenda, which advanced minimum wages, Social Security, welfare, labor standards, and a broad array of economic policies that challenged monopolistic concentrations of wealth. Though himself a nominal Episcopalian, Roosevelt's ideas were heavily influenced by Monsignor John A. Ryan, a populist Catholic priest from Minnesota whose writings on economic justice, labor, and social inequality were widely read in the decades following World War I. In 1919, the U.S. Catholic Bishops tapped Ryan to write their *Program for Social Reconstruction*, a document that Jesuit scholar Joseph M. McShane credited with launching the "American Catholic search for social justice" in earnest. The program called for what at the time were dramatic social reforms: a minimum wage, public housing for workers, labor participation in management decisions, and insurance for illness, disability, unemployment, and the elderly.

In 1931, Pope Pius XI released *Quadragesimo Anno* (The Fortieth Year), an encyclical that included a section ambitiously titled "On Reconstruction of the Social Order." Issued to commemorate the anniversary of Pope Leo XIII's landmark labor encyclical *Rerum Novarum* (On the Condition of Labor), Pius XI offered a stinging critique of unchecked capitalism that resonated far beyond the ecclesial halls of power. That same year, as Lew Daly observed in his article "In Search of the Common Good: The Catholic Roots of American Liberalism," Roosevelt delivered a speech calling for "social justice, through social action," in which he quoted extensively from *Quadragesimo Anno*. In Roosevelt's words:

> It is patent in our days that not alone is wealth accumulated, but immense power and despotic economic domination are concentrated in the hands of a few, and that those few are frequently not the owners but only the trustees and directors of invested funds which they administer at their good pleasure.... This accumulation of power, the characteristic note of the modern economic order, is a natural result of limitless free competition, which permits the survival of those only who are the strongest.

Although we all know that Roosevelt went on to win the election, many of us don't remember that the president asked the man who had influenced so much of his New Deal agenda to give the invocation at his second inauguration. Monsignor Ryan was the first Catholic priest to hold that honor.

So what happened to the Catholic vision of the common good in the public square? In general, the past four decades have witnessed a slow erosion of common good values, along with the decline of community, a rise in corporate power, and the movement of working-class Catholics from the economic margins of American society to a comfortable place in the middle class. The 1980s in particular witnessed the advance of a political philosophy that vilified "big government"—an idea that resonated widely at a time of economic stagnation and gloomy American morale. Indeed, as many Catholics themselves began to realize the American dream, they started to view government less as a protector of basic rights and services for the marginalized and the poor and more as a meddlesome "tax-and-spend" bureaucracy. America also lost the ability to imagine government as a servant of the common good—a deeply Catholic concept.

As we move into the twenty-first century, the realities of both Wall Street and Main Street show us just how divorced we've become from authentic common good values. A 2007 front-page article in the *New York Times*, headlined "The Richest of the Rich, Proud of a New Gilded Age," featured billionaire tycoons who bemoaned taxes on their fortunes and had little to say about why more than thirty-seven million Americans live in poverty in the world's richest country. The NASDAQ exchange launched a private stock market in 2007 for elite investors with assets of more than $100 million. Meanwhile, in many towns and cities, blue-collar jobs that once supported the middle class have disappeared as corporations (many of which are run by our era's new tycoons) pursue cheap labor and higher profits outside the United States. And a commitment to the "commons"—public spaces and resources that benefit all—is being replaced by private gated communities where strangers of different classes or complexions are kept at a comfortable distance.

The U.S. Catholic Bishops emphasize, in addition to many other primary concerns, the enduring power of the common good in their political responsibility statement *Faithful Citizenship*, released ahead of every U.S. presidential election. "Politics in this election year and beyond should be about an old idea with new power—the common good," they wrote in 2003. "The central question should not be, 'Are you better off than you were four years ago?' It should be, 'How can we—all of us, especially the weak and vulnerable—be better off in the years ahead?'" Indeed, this message speaks directly to the excessive individualism that has accompanied American political movements in recent years, including the "Reagan Revolution" and interest-group politics from both sides of the political spectrum.

Our church's long history of grounding the common good in the dignity of the human person and the specific demands of justice makes Catholics especially well suited to challenge our nation's leaders to embrace a more robust common good agenda. No political party has a monopoly on moral values, and both Republicans and Democrats have an equal opportunity to succeed or fail in living up to the obligations of the common good. As Catholics, our faith inspires us to help reshape our culture and serve not as members of just another interest group but as participants in a global church that recognizes our common humanity as children of God. We should take up this struggle with hope, insisting that our public officials treat the common good as the foundation of moral leadership, rather than another catchphrase in a campaign playbook. In this way, Catholics speak from the heart of our tradition with a message as old as the Gospels and as powerfully relevant today as it will be a century from now.

Restoring the Common Good

Building a culture of the common good isn't just something we think of as a theological ideal or the right moral thing to do. It turns out that it's also the smart thing to do—it makes common sense. Statistics confirm what we know intuitively in our own hearts and minds to be true *and* what our Catholic faith tells us: that we are all better off when we look out for the interests of everyone, not just the few. We see the crucial value of the common good when we consider the effect that neglecting it has on *all* Americans.

Challenges to the Common Good

Today's wealth gap poses a serious challenge to the common good. The glaring disparities between wealth and poverty threaten the well-being of everyone—the rich, the poor, and the middle class. CEOs take home over 360 times the pay of average workers, and the richest 1 percent of Americans own 34 percent of the nation's private wealth, more than the combined wealth of the bottom 90 percent, according to United for a Fair Economy. With this kind of extreme wealth gap we all live shorter lives, including the richest Americans. When we abandon the common good, the economy also stagnates, homicide rates increase, more children grow up poor, and charities get less support. And numerous studies, compiled by a project called Extreme Inequality, show that this huge wealth gap isn't good for business either. The last time rich and poor stood this sharply divided was in 1929, right before the stock market crashed, erasing fortunes in the blink of an eye.

Turning our backs on the common good is also dangerous for America's standing in the world and for our national security. It makes us less competitive and it weakens our democracy. After decades of neglecting such common goods as public education, health care, and affordable housing, America is hurting. Our students lag far behind in math and science when compared to students in most European countries, putting our future economic competitiveness at risk. In 2007, according to the Organization for Economic Cooperation and Development and the *Economist* magazine's 2007 *Factbook*, when it comes to infant mortality, abortion rates, poverty, and access to health care, the United States ranks behind most industrialized countries in the European Union. All of these facts offend our patriotism and our faith in the American dream. We can and must do better in order to thrive in a global economy and restore our nation's moral leadership in the world. By rebuilding a culture of the common good here in America, we can live up to our greatness as a country and as a global beacon of hope and freedom.

Building a Culture of the Common Good

How do we build a culture of the common good? First and foremost, we need to put the commandment to love our neighbor into action at all levels of society. We have to restore our nation's rightful balance between vibrant self-reliance and robust concern for one another. We must be prepared to address the problems in our *culture*, including the values and choices that orient our daily lives. We need to stop looking for instant fixes and immediate gratification and take the long view, to start thinking about our own futures and especially those of our children and grandchildren. The common good also requires that we think about how our own lifestyles and patterns of consumption affect those around us.

Although restoring the common good requires that all of us make better individual choices, we are not arguing that building a nation for all is merely an individual or private enterprise. On the contrary, it requires that we look at the function of every structure of society—our politics, our pop culture, our businesses, and all levels of government. We also need leaders who have the courage and conviction to hold these structures to a higher standard, to embrace the notion that in the long run, we all do better when we take care of everyone.

This is no simple task. We live in an increasingly fragmented society in which pervasive corporate and media influences shape a consumer culture that divides us up according to our purchasing preferences, and in which sophisticated advertising campaigns create insatiable appetites for the latest must-have accessories. Corporate branding, twenty-four-hour shopping channels, and aggressive marketing even to toddlers have a significant effect on how Americans view the world.

In his book *Consumed: How Markets Corrupt Children, Infan-tilize Adults, and Swallow Citizens Whole*, Benjamin R. Barber demonstrates how the powerful forces of this consumer culture breed conformity and threaten the essential values of critical thinking and civic engagement. "Once upon a time, capitalism was allied with virtues that also contributed to democracy, respon-sibility, and citizenship," Barber writes. "Today it is allied with vices which—although they serve consumerism—undermine democracy, responsibility, and citizenship." As Americans con-sume more and participate less in civic and political life in their local communities, the foundations of a healthy democracy become weaker. As we'll see in the next chapter, Pope John Paul II challenged a culture of excessive materialism and consumerism, which he blamed for many of our modern social problems.

In 2007, Catholics in Alliance, along with a number of prominent Christian leaders, sponsored a campaign to challenge the commercialization of Christmas and the seasonal Christ-mas pundit, Fox News commentator Bill O'Reilly. O'Reilly, a self-proclaimed culture warrior, wants us to believe that Christ-mas is under seige by secular liberal campaigns to remove religious displays from public places and force us to say "Happy Holidays" instead of "Merry Christmas." But most Americans feel a differ-ent kind of panic and pressure every December: the need to fight snarls of traffic and run around like maniacs to buy the latest and greatest gifts. Christmas itself is supposed to be a gift—a message of hope and peace and love for the poor in the darkest time of the year. It's a time to spend with family and friends and to reach out to neighbors who are suffering. But instead the holiday is often experienced more as a season of shopping that can make or break the U.S. economy. Americans from across the country called to thank us for helping get this message out, and many asked what they could do to help make Christmas a holiday for the common good and good news for the poor.

Strong communities and widespread participation in civic associations were once defining features of American life. Civic engagement swelled after World War II as Elks Lodges, the American Farm Bureau Federation, the Rotary Club, parent-teacher associations, and a host of other men's and women's clubs provided opportunities for people across class lines to gather in community. These groups offered more than networks for socializing. They actively engaged citizens to participate in the process of government and public life. The Veterans of Foreign Wars and the American Legion, for example, were integral in pressuring Congress to pass the G.I. Bill, one of the most important pieces of legislation in our nation's history, which provided college tuition for generations of armed service members. Today, high-priced lobbyists set the agenda in Washington, and the voices of average Americans are rarely heard when it comes to decisions that affect all our lives. Although the G.I. Bill still exists for soldiers who survive their tours in Iraq, a growing number of veterans return home to battle injury and depression.

While public places where diverse groups of citizens once gathered to argue about politics and community activism are harder to find, many Americans are finding ways to rebuild these kinds of networks in new and creative ways. Increasingly, Americans are joining faith- and community-based groups such as the Gamaliel Foundation (http://www.gamaliel.org), PICO—People Improving Communities through Organizing (http://www.piconetwork.org), and ACORN—Association of Community Organizations for Reform Now (http://www.acorn.org). These citizens' groups do heroic work improving our neighborhoods and cities, connecting people of faith with efforts to engage elected officials to expand affordable housing, improve education, and spur economic development.

The incredible popularity of JustFaith (http://www.justfaith. org), a Catholic movement that promotes Catholic social teaching and develops social justice leaders at the parish level, also reveals how eager many people are to work together to build a culture of the common good. We can all participate in these kinds of community efforts—in fact, your own parish or congregation may already be a member of one of these organizations. Ask your pastor or church social justice committee if your parish is involved in such an effort, or check the Web sites mentioned here to find active projects in your part of the country.

While today's increased work hours, longer commutes, and growing financial pressures have left many Americans with less time and energy to be actively engaged in their communities, evidence suggests that we may be reaching a turning point. Neighbors are coming together in new and old forms of community associations. More and more local citizens' organizations are challenging the wisdom of building big-box stores on Main Street, and are encouraging the survival of local businesses. Together we are thinking more about the connections between the things we buy, the people who produce them, and their effect on our health and the environment. Colorful farmers' markets, which make for smart economics and good civics, are becoming common features in suburban and city neighborhoods. These markets help local producers sell their goods directly and more profitably to city and suburban folks, who in turn get healthier, less-expensive, environmentally friendly, and locally grown food. They also serve as important community gathering points, helping neighbors build the bonds necessary for vibrant neighborhoods and real democracy.

The Catholic Church and the broader faith community support this kind of exchange on a global level. Catholic

Relief Services' Fair Trade Program (http://www.crsfairtrade.org) encourages consumers to see how their spending habits affect the global common good by providing access to and information about environmentally sustainable and labor-friendly products. The 2007 uproar over poisonous lead found on toys imported from China drove home the dangers of the alternative: accepting a race to the bottom for the cheapest goods, and a political culture that rejects even minimal government regulation and product safety rules. The bottom line, we are learning, is that the daily decisions we make and the relationships we create as citizens and consumers can help build a culture of the common good and promote and protect human dignity, both in our own communities and around the world.

Rebuilding the Common Good for Our Families, Jobs, and Environment

Our postindustrial consumer culture, in which individual profit has increasingly eclipsed the common good, has placed growing strains on the America family. Real wages (the actual value of the dollars we earn) have declined for years, home ownership is becoming tenuous, and close to half of all marriages end in divorce. Parents worry about the values children are learning from "reality" shows and Hollywood movies that glorify violence and portray sex as a casual activity devoid of commitment or consequences. While our culture often seems to measure success in financial terms alone, many Americans feel they must work longer hours to buy bigger houses, suffering loss of community and extended commutes in the process.

Many families, however, are making different choices. In 2007, the *Washington Post* reported on church-based support groups for families who are trying to live within, and even below, their means in order to resist cultural pressures to buy big and then live strapped for cash. Some parents are working from home when they can in order to spend more time with their children. They are trying to keep their houses and lifestyles smaller and shortening their commutes. But the pressures are still strong. To build a culture of the common good, we need to challenge these cultural pressures and make choices that help keep our families and our society strong. We also need to get our priorities straight. Are having the big house and the fancy car really worth it when the time we spend working for these things keeps us away from our children? A number of Web resources are available to help us begin to shape our everyday lives in ways that won't drain us of time, energy, and money, including http://www.christiansimpleliving.com and http://www.newdream.org. Catholic author Jeff Cavins has also written extensively on living simply; you can find his books at http://www.ascensionpress.com.

The recent mortgage crisis and credit crunch devastated families across the economic spectrum, leaving several million people struggling to keep their homes. To stem the tide of foreclosures, the banks and the government worked out a deal to freeze rates for some homeowners, an essential and appropriate action to protect the common good as well as our economy as a whole. Even before this action, community organizations were lobbying for reform of the kind of predatory lending practices that contributed to the crisis. But certainly the whole problem could have been avoided if a basic understanding of the common good—awareness that what hurts the least among us eventually hurts all of us—had driven our policies in the first place, instead of an unfettered drive for profit on the part of mortgage companies and real estate speculators.

Catholic Charities USA (CCUSA) identifies a shortage of jobs that pay a just wage as a root cause of U.S. poverty and, in their words, a "threat to the common good." They call for more living-wage jobs and an increase in the minimum wage as part of their campaign to reduce poverty here at home. Successful livable-wage initiatives across the country have provided an important model for job creation. When leaders make short-term promises to create new jobs using tax incentives and investments, governments and churches will eventually have to provide assistance to new workers if the new jobs don't pay living wages. We end up paying twice: first in tax breaks or subsidies to companies to create new jobs and second in public or private assistance to those same underpaid workers. These initiatives work to ensure that jobs created with taxpayer dollars pay well to begin with. Meanwhile, membership in unions, which has been integral to ensuring adequate family wages, has declined dramatically since the 1950s. In response, labor leaders are emphasizing new organizing efforts, as well as innovative public-private partnerships in order to create secure jobs and improve workers' lives.

The global climate crisis, one of the most urgent issues of our time, presents us with rich opportunities to build a culture of the common good here in our country and around the world. The reality and impacts of climate change remind us of an essential truth that underlies a commitment to the common good: that our lives are deeply interconnected with others here and around the globe. The cars we drive, the pollution we emit, and the excesses of our consumer lifestyle have tremendous consequences for others. America's carbon emissions disproportionately affect our poorest neighbors in Africa and Asia, who bear the brunt of extreme weather, drought, food shortages, and rising sea levels. The response of our own country and the global community to this crisis is a life-and-death issue for millions around the globe and for the planet as a whole. And failure to act will have dire consequences.

Many Americans are already making better choices: conserving energy at home, driving smaller cars, recycling, and supporting wind and solar energy. Hybrid gasoline-and-electric vehicles are becoming more affordable and more popular. And wind farms are popping up across the country, providing economic benefits to financially pressed farmers (who lease their land and continue farming it) and infusing struggling rural towns with new tax revenues.

But in addition to personal choices, Americans want and need incentives: policies and leaders who will help make these changes more universal and these choices more accessible. We need leaders who will level the economic playing field for clean technologies by making sure that incentives for clean technologies rival those for dirtier technologies. American businesses are also pleading for leadership and calling for certainty about future regulations that they know are both essential and inevitable.

As people of faith, we believe in the kind of moral urgency that inspired movements to end slavery, secure women the vote, and galvanize black and white Americans to confront the sins of racism and bigotry. To build a culture of the common good, we need courageous and creative policies that respond to the urgent moral issues of our time. We need laws to help create more just and equitable social structures and to protect everyone's rights. In Chapter Five, "An Agenda for the Common Good," we will take a deeper look at the role government, law, and public policy can play in restoring our focus on the common good and building a nation for all.

Agape is a Greek word that generally translates as "love." But in Judeo-Christian thought, it is understood more specifically as the selfless, unconditional love that God shows for his children and that we are called to reflect in our own lives. Agape is not a sticky-sweet emotion or vague affection. It's a demanding and redemptive love for our neighbors that challenges us to recognize ourselves and the image of God in all humanity. Jesus explains this most clearly when an expert in the law asks him, "Who is my neighbor?" and he tells the parable of the Good Samaritan who finds a Levite man beaten and left for dead on the side of the road. A priest and another Levite have already passed and ignored the man, but this Samaritan, a foreigner, puts bandages on the man's wounds and takes him to an inn for care. You don't have to be Christian to recognize how that profound teaching speaks to us more than twenty centuries later. You just need enough faith to believe in the common good.

Fortunately, our faith already has a blueprint for action to rebuild the common good. This framework is called the Catholic social tradition, and we'll explore its core message, key themes, and history in the next chapter. The tradition explains how core Catholic values of human dignity and the common good intersect with the problems and possibilities of modern society.

The Catholic Social Tradition

Whether we grow up in a religious family or come to our faith later in life, one thing all Catholics and Christians share is a profound call to love our neighbors as ourselves. This is both an essential teaching of our church and something that many Americans, regardless of religious or political affiliation, feel deep in our hearts. How many times have we as individuals felt closer to God through our families and communities, or by working with the hungry and the poor in spirit? Being Catholic means both having a personal relationship with God and experiencing our faith with others in community.

In a culture that sometimes pressures us to separate our spiritual lives from our social conscience and responsibilities, Catholicism challenges us to bring the two together. Indeed, helping the needy and working with others to build a more just society is every bit as essential to our faith as going to Mass on Sunday. Pope Benedict XVI makes this point often in his writings when he connects social justice with the celebration of Holy Communion—a sacrament that calls to mind our deep connections to others. In short, our responsibility to make the common good and social justice a reality in the world *is* a spiritual vocation.

The Church's teaching about this responsibility has a name: the *Catholic social tradition*. Never heard of it? You're not alone. In the United States, Catholicism often has a distorted reputation for focusing primarily on issues of personal morality and downplaying social concerns, a reputation driven in large part by individuals who foster this perception in order to further a particular political agenda. In reality, the Church embraces a wide mission in the world that includes promoting the full dignity of the human person and tackling such essential issues as workers' rights, poverty, the environment, and war.

The Catholic social tradition is inspired by a primary concern for the dignity of the human person. As Catholics, we believe that we are all created in the image of God and therefore have an inherent and essential worth. We also believe that we are social beings, and as such, can truly thrive only in society. Our church is particularly concerned with ensuring that our social policy promotes both the dignity of all and the common good. These two themes are interdependent. Preserving the dignity of the human person requires a responsibility to the common good, as social realities and structures have a powerful effect on the well-being of the individual. Likewise, promoting the common good requires respect for the dignity of each person at every level of society.

The Catholic social tradition is the official teaching of our church. In fact, in 2004, the Vatican's Pontifical Council for Justice and Peace—the highest office for social justice in the Church—issued an authoritative book on the subject. The *Compendium of the Social Doctrine of the Church* is essentially the Vatican's encyclopedia of the Catholic social tradition. It makes clear that this tradition is fundamental to the Church's mission of preaching the Gospel, an important part of bringing the "good news" of God's universal love to all, especially to the poor and vulnerable. The Catholic social tradition, the *Compendium* reminds us, is "not a privilege, nor [is it] a digression, a convenience or interference."

Surprising or Familiar?

Even in Catholic circles, homilies and commentaries on social justice often begin with the quip that the Catholic social tradition is "one of our church's best-kept secrets." Why does the Church's relevant and sometimes radical commentary on modern economic and social life surprise so many people? As we've noted, in part it's because this teaching doesn't mesh with a popular perception that limits Catholic concerns to issues of personal morality. But these interpretations of our faith ignore the essential connections among problems like poverty and abortion, and fail to remind us that social and economic justice are crucial to protecting the full dignity of the human person. A "consistent ethic of life" message—which embraces our faith's call to protect and promote life at all stages—is an uncomfortable challenge to simple political slogans.

History also explains the lack of focus on the Catholic social tradition. Among other reasons, the Church's firm rejection of excessive individualism, materialism, and other intellectual assumptions of modern political thought—often important critiques, as we'll see—have contributed to a sense of separation between the Church and rest of contemporary society. This popular perception changed dramatically in 1962 when Pope John XXIII convened a historic meeting of Church leaders known as the Second Vatican Council. (The First Vatican Council was held in 1869–1870.) The council turned the tables by *encouraging* Christians to engage the problems of the world in new and creative ways, envisioning that lay people would work to change society as key parts of their spiritual journeys. The division between our everyday life and our spiritual life, Pope John said, was one of the "more serious errors of our age."

Despite the council's reforms, however, it's still true that many American Catholics never hear the words *Catholic*, *social*, and *tradition* in the same sentence. Chris was an altar boy and went through his first three years of Catholic college before he encountered the phrase, and Alexia didn't really get the whole story until she learned about the antipoverty work of the Catholic Campaign for Human Development. But the idea that part of being Catholic means applying the Christian message to the social problems of our world was to both of us, as it is to all who discover the Catholic social tradition, already deeply familiar.

What is this tradition, both surprising and familiar to so many Catholics? First of all, it tends to go by many names. We refer to it in this book as the Catholic social tradition, but it's also called Catholic social teaching, Catholic social doctrine, and even the Catholic social magisterium. The Catholic social tradition has found articulation over the course of more than one hundred years in a series of papal letters known as *social encyclicals*, and in statements by bishops' synods and conferences that address current social, economic, political, and cultural issues. Its inspiration and sources include scripture, philosophy, and the experiences of our community. Throughout Church history, popes have issued letters on social themes, but it was Pope Leo XIII's 1891 publication of *Rerum Novarum* (On the Condition of Labor) that officially launched the "modern" Catholic social tradition. Father Kenneth Himes, a Franciscan priest and theologian, observes in his comprehensive commentary on the tradition, *Modern Catholic Social Teaching*, that this encyclical propelled a broader commitment on the part of the Church to the social questions of the times. But the tradition is not limited to a series of documents alone. It is also a tradition of action, of joining with others to bring the vision of the documents to life.

Insofar as the Catholic social tradition builds on the past and responds to new realities, it is in fact a *tradition* in the deepest sense of the word, developing with each successive generation and expanding on earlier themes. But in addition to being traditional—as one might expect the Catholic Church to be, valuing and building on past precepts and principles—it is also profoundly *countercultural*. It consistently challenges the assumptions of society as a whole and calls our world to an ever-deepening sense of the common good.

The tradition provides a consistent critique of the dominant philosophical and political theories of the past several centuries. It challenges, as we noted earlier, the excessive individualism of today's conservative and liberal movements, both of which can trace their ancestry to the materialism of Enlightenment philosophy. And while certain activists would like to diminish government to the point at which it's small enough, in the words of Americans for Tax Reform's Grover Norquist, to "drown in a bathtub," the Catholic social tradition insists that government must play an essential role in promoting the common good, particularly to protect the interests of the poor and vulnerable.

At the same time, the Catholic social tradition affirms the need for reasonable restraints on government activity through a principle called "subsidiarity." This concept broadly asserts that while government must ensure the common good, social issues and decisions should be addressed at the level most appropriate to the problem at hand and closest to the parties affected. The Catholic social tradition takes both communism and capitalism to task, leveling their assumptions about human nature, markets, and the relationship between individuals and society. The fact that the Catholic social tradition echoes the Gospels' ancient call to put the poor first shapes its countercultural critique of many of today's reigning economic and political assumptions, including the notion that free markets alone can ensure a just and equitable society, and an excessive individualism that neglects any responsibility for society as a whole.

Key Themes of the Catholic Social Tradition

Because of its broad scope, the Catholic social tradition is often distilled to a more manageable listing of key themes or principles. Scholars have proposed different formulations, which vary from seven to fifteen or more themes. The Vatican's *Compendium*, for example, identifies four "permanent principles": the dignity of the human person, solidarity, subsidiarity, and the common good. The U.S. Catholic Bishops present seven key themes of Catholic social teaching in their political responsibility statements and in other educational materials. Father Bill Byron, in his frequently cited 1998 article in *America* magazine, presents the "Ten Building Blocks of Catholic Social Teaching."

And Todd Whitmore, in *Living the Catholic Social Tradition*, presents six themes, starting with the "common good" in order to emphasize both the social nature of the person and the tradition's consistent challenge to the excessive individualism of much of modern Western thought.

The ten core themes we list here emerge from our own visit in this chapter with some of the tradition's key popes and their encyclicals, and from the Vatican's *Compendium of the Social Doctrine of the Church*.

The Dignity of the Human Person

The Catholic social tradition is grounded in the Christian belief that each of us is created in the image of God and that we therefore share an intrinsic and sacred dignity. In this respect, it is absolutely essential that society be ordered to protect and promote the *dignity of each human person*—young or old, guilty or innocent, born or unborn. We must, in the words of the *Gaudium et Spes* (the Second Vatican Council's Pastoral Constitution on the Church in the Modern World) "consider every neighbor without exception as another self, taking into account first of all his life and the means necessary for living it with dignity."

The Common Good

The *common good* stands at the center of the Catholic social tradition and calls us to understand that loving our neighbors as ourselves ranks among the highest of Christian virtues. This call is essential to building healthy and productive societies, as well as our own personal well-being. Only when our society provides essential conditions like health care, jobs, education, and opportunity, our church teaches, can we reach our full human potential. We are by nature social beings, and as such, society's purpose is to serve the whole human person at every level—through government, economy, and culture. According to the *Catechism of the Catholic Church*, the common good is the very "reason that the political authority exists." The common good demands peace, justice, care for the environment, and essential rights and services such as food, housing, basic health care, education, work, and religious freedom.

Solidarity

The principle of *solidarity* encourages us to see our membership in one global family, sharing a common humanity and profound interdependence with all persons and especially with individuals who are living in poverty. The *Compendium* notes that solidarity is a moral and social virtue that determines the right order of institutions and as such demands that we transform structures of sin into structures of solidarity through the creation of just laws and fair market regulations. Solidarity requires that we support human rights, workers' rights, fair trade, and integral human development. Pope John Paul II insisted that "development and liberation takes concrete shape in the exercise of solidarity, that is to say in the love and service of neighbor, especially of the poorest."

Subsidiarity

The Catholic social tradition strongly affirms the essential and positive role government plays in promoting human dignity and the common good. The tradition also recognizes that *effective* government is that which serves the people on the most local level possible. In addition to ensuring efficiency and familiarity with the problems of modern society, this notion of *subsidiarity* frees larger government entities to focus on challenges that manifest on a national or international scale and on supportive and coordinating functions. Indeed, subsidiarity's Latin root, *subsidere*, literally means "to support." Global issues like peacemaking, environmental stewardship, and broad efforts to stimulate national economies are appropriate to such high-level functions. But services like fire, police, and public schools are fit for local government entities, which best understand the particular needs of their citizens.

The Preferential Option for the Poor

Catholics believe that the fundamental measure of any society or economy is the health and welfare of those who are most vulnerable. Jesus calls us to a special concern for the poor, and in the Catholic social tradition, the *preferential option for the poor* requires that we make a top priority of changing structures that perpetuate poverty. All levels of government accept a chief responsibility to promote the interests of the poor, but according to the principle of subsidiarity, people living in poverty must also be key agents of change in any structural and individual solutions. Concern for the poor is a value that speaks to the very foundation of Christianity. According to the *Compendium*, "The Church's social doctrine, in consideration of the privilege accorded by the Gospel to the poor, repeats over and over that 'the more fortunate should renounce some of their rights so as to place their goods more generously at the service of others.'"

The Dignity of Work and the Rights of Workers

Because each human person has inherent dignity independent of his or her economic value, work is designed to benefit the person, not the other way around. Work is a way in which we participate in God's ongoing creation and express our unique vocations as human beings; it is, as the *Compendium* reminds us, "a fundamental right and a good for mankind." As such, a concern for the *dignity of work and the rights of workers* must ground any social or economic program. In this era of economic globalization, it is all the more important to remember that people should always take priority over profit. Workers, in the Catholic social tradition, have essential human rights: to a just and living wage that will support workers' families, to organize and bargain collectively through trade unions, to safe and to humane working conditions, and to leisure time to spend with their friends and families. Employees have a responsibility to hold up their end of the bargain, but so too must employers take an active role in protecting these essential rights.

Rights, Responsibilities, Participation

The Catholic social tradition teaches that all human beings have both *a right and a responsibility to participate* in the economic, political, and cultural life of society. Our personal and political decisions must be made with an eye toward the well-being of our families and the entire global human community, and a just society cannot exist where the rights to life and material prosperity are not available to all. Preserving our rights requires all of us to be actively involved in the processes of society and government. According to the *Catechism of the Catholic Church*, "Participation is a duty to be fulfilled consciously by all, with responsibility and with a view to the common good."

Universal Destination of Goods

Because God created the resources of the earth for the common use of all human beings, these resources must be utilized in ways that benefit everyone, not just the few. In the Catholic social tradition, this concept is known as the *universal destination of goods*. Our church teaches that private property has an important social function, but only when it serves the common good. Excessive materialism and consumerism—in which acquisition of wealth and power take priority over sharing the resources we hold in common—violates this principle. These "structural sins" entrap people in lifestyles that erode their spiritual and physical well-being and degrade the natural environment; the solution is to focus on *being more* rather than *having more*. According to the Vatican II document *Gaudium et Spes*, the universal destination of goods means that "the right to have a share of earthly goods sufficient for oneself and one's family belongs to everyone."

Stewardship of God's Creation

Much as the principle of the universal destination of goods speaks to the human right to share in the fruits of the earth, the Catholic social tradition's call to *stewardship of God's creation* emanates from our belief that our natural environment is a gift from God. At a time in history when the world is waking up to the realities of human-induced climate change, the need to care for the earth is becoming clearer by the day. Effective stewardship of creation speaks to principles at the very heart of our faith; John Paul II noted that "care for the environment . . . is a matter of a common and universal duty, that of respecting the common good." Governments and the international community have a positive responsibility to protect the environment and to prevent destruction of the atmosphere and the biosphere. In both our public policy and personal lives, we must work to preserve our forests, ensure clean water, promote renewable energy sources, and protect species and biodiversity.

Peace

Our faith requires us to work to foster *peace* at all levels of society. Peace is not merely the absence of war. It is the product of justice and concern for the dignity of all human persons. The Catholic social tradition teaches that peace on earth is possible only when we work to promote the common good and the welfare of all peoples. We must pursue alternatives to war, the arms race, nuclear proliferation, and other weapons of mass destruction. Our military spending should be reallocated to reduce poverty and meet social needs. We must also oppose economic injustice and corruption, which are often the roots of conflict and violence. The *Compendium* asserts that finding "alternative solutions to war" and seeking "out the causes underlying bellicose conflicts, especially those connected with structural situations of injustice, poverty, and exploitation" are essential to building a culture of the common good.

Popes and Principles

The Catholic social tradition is too expansive to address its entire history in this book. But over the years, some of the writings and work of our church leaders have stood out in particular as significant steps forward in the development of social doctrine. Here we look at several of these popes and examine some of their key encyclicals in order to get a better sense of how the core themes of the Catholic social tradition develop in the face of changing social and economic realities.

The Workers' Pope: Leo XIII

Pope Leo XIII's 1891 encyclical *Rerum Novarum* (On the Condition of Labor) officially launched the Church's social tradition by addressing the dramatic economic and social upheavals that accompanied the Industrial Revolution. Although industrialization is what made our modern society possible, it also took a terrible toll on human dignity, introducing or exacerbating modern social problems such as child labor, sweatshops, displaced families, urban poverty, and disease. The traditional economic guild system and rural lifestyle were rapidly disappearing as agricultural workers moved to urban factories and a new opposition between factory owners (often known as "capital") and their laborers developed along with an increasingly massive gap between rich and poor.

Pope Leo insisted that securing the rights of workers was a key solution to this real human suffering and to the "labor question"—what the encyclical calls the central social issue of the day. Workers have a right to a family wage (which meant at the time that a father had to earn enough to provide adequately for his family), a right to strike, and a right to organize into worker associations—precursors to today's unions. Child labor, according to Leo, is completely unacceptable. Since few of these rights were legally established at the time of *Rerum Novarum*, the encyclical placed the Church on the cutting edge of progress on these issues.

Rerum Novarum helped transform the dominant understanding of poverty at the time. Challenging the popular notion that poverty was the result of personal moral failings alone, Pope Leo asserted that it was also caused by unjust economic and social systems. In the late nineteenth century, Marxism was gaining traction among distressed and exploited workers, but Pope Leo challenged its proposition of class warfare, instead offering the solution of "class cooperation"—productive alliances between workers and owners. This challenge of cooperation would become the robust principle of solidarity described in later papal letters.

Firmly planting the common good at the beginning of the tradition, the letter makes clear that serving the needs of all citizens is not only a duty of government but the very reason for government's existence. Even today, the basic conviction that government exists to serve the common good and to promote the interests of all challenges the "no government is good government" dogma espoused by both libertarians and "neoconservatives." Pope Leo, in contrast, ties the role of government to the promotion of everyone's interests, especially those living in poverty, in an early expression of the preferential option for the poor: "It lies in the power of a ruler to benefit every class in the State," Leo wrote, "and amongst the rest to promote to the utmost the interests of the poor; and this in virtue of his office ... since it is the province of the commonwealth to serve the common good."

The Social Justice Pope: Pius XI

Four decades after *Rerum Novarum*, amid the global economic crisis that began in 1929, Pope Pius XI issued his 1931 encyclical, appropriately titled *Quadragesimo Anno* (The Fortieth Year). At a time when communism, fascism, and international financial entities were rising in influence, Pius undertook an expansion of several key principles of the Catholic social tradition. He strengthened the Church's commitment to solidarity with workers and its condemnation of the gap between rich and poor. His encyclical also reaffirmed a worker's right to organize a union and to earn a family wage. Dismissing the charge—coming even from some Catholics—that workers' associations were inherently instruments of socialism, Pius hailed the enactment of civil labor laws since *Rerum Novarum*. He also called for greater worker participation in ownership and management, a theme that would find further development in future encyclicals.

Like Pope Leo, Pius believed that an essential and primary role of government is to promote the common good. He has strong words for both socialism and capitalism, and insists that government play some positive role in reigning in the unbridled free market to ensure economic justice and fairness. *Quadragesimo Anno* introduced the concept of social justice, which, Pius writes, demands closing the gap between the rich and poor and instituting a broader sharing in economic progress.

Pope Pius also introduced the key social principle of subsidiarity, which, as we have seen, both affirms the notion that government entities closest to particular problems can find the most effective solutions and creates a clear role for larger governmental functions. As we noted earlier, subsidarity's Latin root, *subsidere*, literally means "to support." And as Todd Whitmore observes, according to subsidiarity, larger government entities must support essential public functions that local entities cannot always adequately provide, such as security and transportation infrastructure. Subsidiarity, Pius insists, does not absolve government from its responsibility to ensure the common good and the interests of all; rather, it more clearly defines the positive role government can play as an agent of social change. In this spirit, the Catholic social tradition also repeatedly calls for world leaders to strengthen international institutions that promote global peace and solidarity.

A Pope for the Common Good: John XXIII

In the late 1960s, as we discussed previously, Pope John XXIII initiated a pivotal moment in the history of the Catholic Church. The Second Vatican Council, commonly known as Vatican II, brought bishops, priests, women religious, and theologians from around the world together in Rome to examine the Church and its role in the world. Pope John sought to turn the Church to greater international engagement—a timely move, as the former colonies of Europe were emerging as independent nations and global economic injustice and threats of nuclear war loomed large on the horizon. Hailing from poor peasant roots himself, John had been exposed at a young age to family members and Church leaders who stood with the poor in practical ways. As Professor Marvin Mich notes in *Modern Catholic Social Teaching*, when John was a young priest, his bishop emphasized Christ's "preference" for the poor and supported striking workers. And the future pope's experience as a chaplain in World War I would ultimate lead him to brand war "the greatest evil."

John XXIII takes the common good to a global level in his key encyclicals, *Mater et Magistra* (Christianity and Social Progress) and *Pacem in Terris* (Peace on Earth). As *America* editor Father Drew Christiansen notes in his commentary in *Modern Catholic Social Teaching*, *Pacem in Terris* coins the concept of the "universal common good," in which our ultimate social concerns consider the good of the entire world community. Like the popes before him, John insisted that the very purpose of government is to promote the common good.

Recognizing the increasing complexity of modern society, Pope John made a new case for an expanded role of the state, particularly in economic matters. He outlines several specific activities that the government should consider in order to promote the common good, including steps to maximize employment and employee ownership, increased state regulation of corporate directors, some degree of price controls, and enhanced social security. John is vehement in his belief that market forces alone will not truly promote the common good, and he is equally critical of the tendency of both Marxism and capitalism to violate Christian principles of solidarity and human dignity. A clear understanding of the common good and the principles of solidarity and subsidiarity, he insists, should shape any government intervention.

Engaging the World: Vatican II

The Second Vatican Council inaugurated an era of increased Church engagement with society and culture. The council issued four major "constitutions" that emphasize the social role of the Church and call for a renewed focus on scripture and spirituality. Vatican II took place during the Cold War and an accelerating global arms race, notes Jesuit scholar David Hollenbach in *Modern Catholic Social Teaching*. Although the memory of two world wars and the Holocaust was still fresh in the minds of many, humanity was finding new hope in cooperative institutions like the United Nations and in the U.S. struggle for racial equality.

Gaudium et Spes (Joy and Hope, also known as the Pastoral Constitution on the Church in the Modern World) was issued on the last day of the council in 1965. As Father Hollenbach notes, it is one of the most authoritative and significant documents of the Catholic social tradition in the twentieth century. Its title comes from a line in the document that profoundly communicates the principle of solidarity, a bolder expression of the earlier theme of cooperation between classes: "the joys and hopes, the grief and anguish of the people of our time, especially those who are poor and afflicted," the document reads, "are the joys and hopes, the grief and anguish of the followers of Christ." Solidarity, it insists, calls us to confront the scandalous global gap between rich and poor, which violates the principles of social justice and human dignity. To remedy this scandal, *Gaudium et Spes* asks readers to move beyond a morality grounded in individualism to one rooted in community. The notion of freedom also moves beyond the individual to a more communal understanding. Simply put, we become truly free in acting on our responsibility to others.

The Human Development Pope: Paul VI

Forty years before the Irish rock star Bono launched his now-famous ONE Campaign against global poverty, Pope Paul VI called for urgent action to resolve the crisis of global poverty. *Populorum Progressio* (The Development of Peoples) was issued during a period of massive expansion of international trade and the global economy and promoted "integral" human development for poorer nations. While the United States and other developed countries enjoyed robust economic expansion, developing countries struggled to enjoy the benefits of development, especially as many emerged from colonial rule.

Challenging the very definition of development for both wealthy and poor nations in a vehement critique of materialism, Pope Paul maintains that economic and social development cannot be simply about accumulating more things. He insists that "integral" human development requires full social, economic, spiritual, and educational development for all people. The related principle of the universal destination of goods holds that the products of society are intended for the benefit of everyone and requires placing some reasonable limits on unrestrained competition and private property. According to this principle, people must have access to the resources and conditions required for full human development. Pope Paul also coins the powerful phrase "development is the new name for peace," affirming that peace requires economic justice, not just the absence of war.

Pope Paul calls wealthy nations to three responsibilities: solidarity, social justice, and universal charity. Solidarity requires generous foreign aid to poorer nations, while social justice requires ending unfair trade practices and other structures of oppression. Pope Paul also affirms the role the United Nations and other international institutions can play in bringing these ideals to life on a global scale. Issuing a strong challenge to the rich, he asks if wealthy individuals are prepared to step up to pay higher taxes for more development aid, or to pay more for imported goods—a possible consequence of fairer trade relations.

The Life and Social Justice Pope: John Paul II

Many Americans remember John Paul II as the pope who brought the abstract notions of solidarity and social justice to life through his support for democratic movements in the former Soviet Union and the Solidarity movement in Poland. John Paul also introduced the concept of a "culture of life" and its powerful call to our consciences and to society to lovingly protect all human beings. Biographers have pointed out that John Paul's own experience living behind the Iron Curtain shaped a passion for social justice and human rights, as well as his critique of both communism and capitalism.

Four of Pope John Paul's most significant encyclicals emphasize the centrality of human dignity to the Catholic social tradition. *Laborem Exercens* (On Human Work) in 1981, *Sollicitudo Rei Socialis* (On Social Concern) in 1987, and *Centesimus Annus* (On the Hundredth Anniversary) in 1991, harken back strongly to the message of *Rerum Novarum*. *Evangelium Vitae* (The Gospel of Life) in 1995 powerfully articulates the Church's commitment to promoting human life at all stages. John Paul brings to maturity several key themes of the Catholic social tradition, including human dignity, the dignity of work, and a concern for the natural environment. He urgently condemns the alarming global gap between rich and poor and first articulates the Church's concern for the poor as a "preferential option for the poor."

Laborem Exercens develops a spiritual understanding of labor, grounding work and the rights of workers in the belief that through our labor we express our human dignity and participate in the ongoing act of creation. The Catholic concept of human dignity affirms that each and every one of us has value independent of our productivity in the market. This also means that human work is intended to benefit the worker, not the other way around.

On Social Concern surveys a range of social and economic problems, including international debt, illiteracy, and the lack of affordable housing. John Paul insists that the Catholic social tradition is critical of the notion that either capitalism or Marxism can fully or effectively provide solutions to these challenges. The scandal of poverty, he believes, requires that we act both personally and globally to put the option for the poor into action. Among these global actions are promoting international fair trade and redirecting military funding (which he calls an "enemy of development") toward poverty alleviation.

In *Evangelium Vitae*, John Paul makes a passionate appeal to love and protect human life. Acknowledging the many threats to life, including poverty, war, the arms trade, and ecological destruction, he focuses primarily on contemporary threats to life at its beginning and end—namely abortion, euthanasia, and embryonic interventions. Because human life is a gift from God, we must lovingly protect it at all stages; hence abortion and euthanasia, John Paul argues, are never morally acceptable. In addition to transforming society to promote life, he notes that "it is not enough to remove unjust laws." He goes on to state that "the underlying attacks on life have to be eliminated, especially by ensuring proper support for family and motherhood." Serious responsibility, the pope believes, lies with "those who should have ensured, but did not, effective family and social policies in support of families." John Paul calls for a cultural transformation that encourages us to value people over things and *being* more human over *having* more possessions. Only when we rediscover a reverence and awe for every human person and grasp the gratuitous nature of life can we replace our modern society's "culture of death" with a "culture of life."

John Paul reaffirms the Catholic conviction that government must take responsibility for advancing the common good. He expands this principle to include concern for both the natural environment and the human environment, which, he insists in *Centesimus Annus*, will not be safeguarded simply by market forces. Just as the state protects workers' rights, today it must also defend common goods such as the natural world, which we all need in order to survive and flourish. Individuals, he insists, must take concrete action on this front as well. Challenging some of the core values of consumerism, John Paul links modern-day environmental crises to the consumer culture of "superdeveloped" countries. It's fine to want to live better, he says, but a lifestyle focused more on *acquiring* than on *being* leads to excess consumption of the earth's resources. This kind of excessive materialism hurts our spiritual and physical health and harms the planet too.

The Pope of Love and Hope: Benedict XVI

Pope Benedict XVI released his encyclical *Deus Caritas Est* (God Is Love) in an uncertain era of war, terrorism, and fear. Deeply theological and scriptural, the 2006 letter surprised and heartened many people with its simple message and meditative tone. It focuses on the message of God's love for us and our reciprocal responsibility to love our neighbors as ourselves. At a time when war, abortion, climate change, and terrorism are urgent global issues that threaten human life and dignity, Pope Benedict insists that in Jesus' parables, the notion of "neighbor" extends far beyond our community and our country. In addition to a deep theological exploration on the nature of love, Pope Benedict elaborates on the Church's responsibility to practice love of neighbor concretely: "love must be organized," he writes, if it is to serve the community. This organization and service occurs through the many initiatives to combat poverty and other social problems.

While the aim of all politics is justice, Pope Benedict calls out "the dazzling effect of power and special interests" that inhibits politics from achieving justice. Here, he demonstrates, is where politics meets faith. Because our human "reason" in politics can be blinded by the influence of interest groups, high-priced lobbyists, and the temptations of power and self-interest, faith aims to "help purify reason" and to "form consciences" to help attain justice.

The encyclical makes clear that the Church should not be viewed as a replacement for the state. Whereas the world of politics is clearly and directly responsible for just structures and laws, the Church's unique role is to reawaken "moral forces" without which justice in the long run is neither established nor effective. While the boundary between church and state is clear, the Church doesn't just "sit on the sidelines in the fight for justice." Government, Benedict insists, is primarily responsible for justice through its laws, the judiciary, and executive leadership; the Church, on the other hand, exists to contribute to "the promotion of justice" as measured by the common good. Indeed, "efforts to bring about an openness of mind and will to the demands of the common good [are] something which concerns the Church deeply."

Individual Catholics, however, are a different story. While delineating a clear boundary between church and state in politics, Benedict emphasizes the individual's direct responsibility to participate in public life, on behalf of justice and the common good. Individuals cannot opt out from the messiness of politics or public life, nor can they "relinquish their participation in the many different economic, social, legislative, administrative and cultural areas, which are intended to promote organically and institutionally the *common good*."

In other writings and talks, Pope Benedict has vehemently denounced extreme poverty, war, and all violent conflicts. In 2007, he noted that "nothing positive comes from Iraq" and called for an end to "all armed conflicts that are bloodying the earth" and to the illusion that using force is the best way to solve conflict. In a 2007 apostolic exhortation called *Sacramentum Caritatis*, Pope Benedict, like his predecessor John Paul II, notes that channeling half of military expenditures to other priorities could "liberate the poor and destitute." He has also called for action to address threats to the environment and expressed particular concern for their effect on the poor.

In his 2007 encyclical *Spe Salvi* (Saved by Hope), Benedict discusses salvation and the hope offered by Christianity in light of contemporary culture. Like Pope John XXIII did in the 1960s, he challenges any attempt to purge the Gospels of their social meaning and firmly links salvation to a broader responsibility "for the whole" and to serving others. "How could the idea have developed that Jesus' message is narrowly individualistic and aimed only at each person singly?" he asks. "How did we arrive at this interpretation of the 'salvation of the soul' as a flight from responsibility for the whole, and how did we come to conceive the Christian project as a selfish search for salvation which rejects the idea of serving others?"

Living the Catholic Social Tradition

The Catholic social tradition is not just a theory; it is also a tradition of action. How do we, as lay Catholics, go about living the Catholic social tradition? How do we participate actively in society to promote justice and the common good, as Pope Benedict urges, and express our responsibility for "the whole"? This is the challenge that drives the efforts of both of our organizations—Catholics United and Catholics in Alliance for the Common Good. The entire U.S. Catholic social justice movement and myriad Catholic organizations, efforts, and initiatives work every day to realize the vision of the Catholic social tradition.

Pope John XXIII urged young people in particular to move the tradition from the abstract to reality. In his encyclical *Mater et Magistra* (Christianity and Social Progress), he offered a straightforward three-part method—"see, judge, act"—to apply Catholic social teaching to real social concerns. It works like this: first, we use our intellect to observe current social reality and events—for example, climate change or poverty. This observation phase is also called "reading the signs of the times." Next, we judge social problems in light of the Gospels and key principles such as human dignity or the common good. Finally, we determine what actions we can take to address the problem effectively.

Pope John was careful to acknowledge the difficulties we face in applying faith to social action, including our culture's excessive materialism, self-interest, and the difficulty in charting the right approach. For example, we can observe the current reality of environmental pollution and climate change, and we can judge it as violating the requirement to care for creation and protect human dignity. But taking effective action, both personally and globally, is often hindered by the self-interest and materialism that pervade our society today. In Chapter Five, "An Agenda for the Common Good," we use this same method, "see, judge, act," to recommend policy actions in light of today's urgent social realities.

The Catholic social tradition is the foundation and inspiration for many national and international Catholic social justice institutions. In 1998, the U.S. Catholic Bishops approved a resolution encouraging better integration of the Catholic social tradition into Catholic education at all levels. Many Catholic colleges and universities, dioceses, and parishes run programs and initiatives that put the tradition into action. The option for the poor, solidarity, and the common good guide the missions of the Catholic Campaign for Human Development (CCHD, the

U.S. Catholic Bishops' domestic antipoverty initiative), Catholic Relief Services, Catholic hospitals and schools, Catholic Charities USA, Caritas Internationalis, a variety of European Catholic relief and development agencies, and state, diocesan, and parish social ministry programs.

Alexia coedited a 2004 book with Georgetown University professor Kathleen Maas Weigert, called *Living the Catholic Social Tradition*, which explores how community leaders throughout the United States are putting their faith into action in innovative and effective ways. It looks at a number of organizations across the country—mainly funded by CCHD—that bring the Catholic social tradition to life each and every day. Putting the dignity of work and the option for the poor into practice, farmworkers in Immokalee, Florida, fought and finally won a national battle with Taco Bell to raise the wages of tomato pickers, who hadn't had a pay increase in more than twenty years. And Baltimoreans United in Leadership Development (BUILD) ran one of the first successful living-wage campaigns in Baltimore.

NETWORK, a national Catholic social justice lobby, was founded by women religious in the 1970s to promote a number of legislative issues of concern to the Catholic social tradition. The Jesuits launched the Washington, D.C.–based Center of Concern that same decade as a Catholic social teaching and global justice think tank. Pax Christi USA focuses on building a peaceful world, addressing racism and the root causes of global conflict.

And since 1975, the National Conference of Catholic Bishops, now called the United States Conference of Catholic Bishops, has issued a statement on political responsibility for Catholic citizens in advance of each presidential election year. The 2007 statement, *Forming Consciences for Faithful Citizenship: A Call to Political Responsibility from the Catholic Bishops in the United States*, is an excellent example of a contemporary application of the Catholic social tradition to current social and political issues. The document applies John XXIII's "see, judge, act" method by reading the current signs of the times and judging them in light of the Gospels and the social tradition.

The affirmative and urgent message of the Catholic social tradition is particularly inspiring and surprising to young people who have often experienced Catholicism as a rule-based faith. As Alexie Torres Fleming, founder of a South Bronx youth justice and peace ministry inspired by Catholic social teaching, noted in *Living the Catholic Social Tradition*, "The great thing about Catholic social teaching is that it's all written in the affirmative. It doesn't say 'you shouldn't do this.' Rather it affirms things, the dignity of human life, the dignity of work, solidarity.... We are constantly acting in the affirmative ... and the main thing that pushes you is the positive force and vision."

In the next chapter, "Church and State," we look at the unique and important American experience of charting an affirmative, fruitful, and appropriate relationship among religious traditions and the world of democratic politics. We also explore the Catholic understanding of these ideas and address some contemporary concerns regarding the relationship between religion and government.

Church and State

As the Evangelical leader Jim Wallis observes in his book *God's Politics: Why the Right Gets It Wrong and the Left Doesn't Get It*, the two things you are not supposed to talk about in polite company are religion and politics.

Like Jim, we've chosen the most "impolite" route possible. Not only do we spend much of our lives talking about these two often-controversial subjects in whatever company will listen, but we talk about both at the same time. The culture war has only deepened the divisions among Americans over the relationship between faith and politics in our country. So it's no wonder that we often find ourselves the target of more than our fair share of criticism.

The culture warriors want us to think in terms of black and white, and where religion and politics are concerned, it's particularly a case of all or nothing. One side tells us that mixing faith and public life violates a treasured American tradition of separation between church and state. The other side claims that by suggesting Catholics should be *prudential* in how they apply their faith to politics, we are diminishing our church's core moral teachings.

As with many aspects of the culture war, not only are both sides missing the point when it comes to the relationship between church and state, but they are generally out of touch with the majority of Americans. Most people we work with—especially those outside the Washington Beltway—value the appropriate division between religion and politics. But at the same time, folks *want* a political dialogue that's rooted in values, including religious values. More than anything, they desire a civil debate that respects a diversity of traditions and differing points of view.

So why the disconnect between the culture warriors and the rest of America? In large part, it's because of the all-or-nothing attitude of the culture war itself. Each side, by taking its respective position to unhealthy extremes, has contributed to a deep-seated mistrust in the other. Some conservatives, for example, have offended millions by using religion as a justification for the Iraq War and by unquestioningly supporting claims that our country's involvement in the Middle East somehow fulfills God's will. And they see no problem with imposing religious tests on candidates and voters—particularly Catholic candidates and voters. Some still claim that America is a "Christian nation," and that what our founders really intended in drafting the Constitution was for Americans to be governed by biblical rather than secular laws. It's no wonder that the millions of non-Christian Americans—and millions of Christians who aren't comfortable with this kind of blurring of the church-state boundary—have come to view such approaches to faith and public life with considerable suspicion.

Progressives have also done their part to alienate people of faith. Scarcely a year goes by without someone, somewhere, challenging a local government's right to fund a holiday display, and all too often we hear stories of lawsuits against public school districts for allowing voluntary—not mandatory, but voluntary—prayer at school events. Some openly decry any reference to personal faith by elected leaders; others litter the Internet with offensive comments about religious traditions, often aimed particularly at the Catholic faith. All this has left a lot of people of faith feeling looked down upon by members of the "secular left," many of whom treat churchgoers as dinosaurs who just need to get with the times.

Both sides have their points, but both have taken them way too far. It's true that our nation's founders were Christians and that faith has throughout our nation's history played an important role in politics and civil society. But it's also true that the founders knew well the danger posed to society and to religion by government-controlled churches and church-controlled government. So in drafting the Constitution and the Bill of Rights, our forefathers knew it was essential to build a system to protect one from the other. These protections were particularly welcome to Catholics in America, as they ensured the freedom for the Church to be the Church and for Catholics to share in the process of government, rights that were *not* guaranteed in the Old World.

The bitter fights that have emerged recently in our own church community are particularly disheartening. Most Catholics understand that separating religion and government is a good thing; it's part of what makes our nation successful and unique, and it's indispensable to preserving our freedom to worship and believe as we please. It's also a principle that dates back to the earliest days of our church.

But sadly, a handful of well-funded partisan operatives have chosen to throw this distinction out the window, at great disservice to our nation and to our church's teachings. For Catholics and for all Americans, the separation between church and state set by the founders is in greater jeopardy now than any other time in history. And what a tragedy this is. The United States is in many ways the most enduring example of democracy the world has ever seen. But it is also in many ways the most fragile. Without constant dialogue, attention, and evaluation, we can easily lose sight of our values and become complacent about the importance of religious freedom to our nation's past and future success.

Just what does the "separation of church and state" mean in the American and Catholic traditions, and how can Catholics participate in a democratic and pluralistic society while remaining faithful to the teachings of their church? Most important, how can Americans of all religious backgrounds find ways to work together to promote the common good? In this chapter, we take up these vital questions and examine the rightful role of faith in the American political system.

The Truth About Separation

"Congress shall make no law respecting an establishment of religion," begins the First Amendment of the U.S. Constitution, "or prohibiting the free exercise thereof." These sixteen words remain today among the most important and most controversial parts of our nation's founding document. For some, they represent a complete prohibition against mixing faith and public life. For others, the fact that many of the Constitution's framers were themselves regular churchgoers is evidence that the Bill of Rights' caution against mixing religion and politics should be applied sparingly at best.

Together these words are known as the *establishment* and *free exercise clauses*, and in the context of the times in which they were written, they made an awful lot of sense. We all know that the Pilgrims sailed to the New World to escape religious persecution. But in many places in colonial America, taxes still went to fund Puritan churches, and preaching the "wrong" religious ideas was still a criminal offense that carried harsh punishments—including death. The American Revolution was fought in part to secure freedom of worship and freedom from the English crown's authority over who could practice what religion and where. In creating a new independent nation, the framers wanted to make sure that Congress could neither *establish* a government-sponsored religion (or tell you what faith to practice, if any) nor deny your right to *exercise* freely whatever religion you choose.

However clear the establishment and free exercise clauses may seem to us today, scholars and the courts have interpreted their legal status in different ways through the years. Many Americans take for granted the notion of "separation of church and state." But actually, this phrase does not appear in the Constitution at all. The first reference to it is found in Thomas Jefferson's 1802 letter to the Danbury Baptists, in which the president referred to a "wall of separation" between religion and government. It wasn't until 1878 that the U.S. Supreme Court would even reference the term and not until 1947 when "separation of church and state" would be debated as a legal principle in a Supreme Court decision.

Despite the Constitution's clear federal prohibition against church-state collusion, it would take more than a century for state governments to be held to the antiestablishment and free exercise standards. Thus Massachusetts had legally collected taxes from its citizens to fund the Congregational Church until 1833—effectively establishing an official state religion. And despite free exercise protections, we still don't have the right to do whatever we want in the name of religion. Over the years, the courts have ruled that if a law that applies to all Americans generally happens to restrict a religious practice along with secular instances of that same conduct, it *can* be considered constitutional. Religion is not a good excuse for taking multiple spouses, for example, and employers can fire workers who use illegal drugs in religious rituals.

A law that specifically targets religious practices, though, will be declared unconstitutional unless the government has a compelling justification for the regulation. So states can't penalize Seventh-day Adventists who refuse to work on the Sabbath. And communities can't pass laws prohibiting animal sacrifice purely to keep adherents to the Santeria faith (which does practice such rituals) out of a neighborhood that just doesn't want Santeria members.

Unfortunately, the courts will at times make free exercise decisions we don't agree with, and living in a pluralist democracy means that we won't always get our way. Catholic Charities of New York, for example, requested an exemption to a 2007 state law requiring all employers to fund contraceptives in employee health benefits. But the U.S. Supreme Court let the legislation stand, even though Catholic organizations and businesses feared this would force them to participate in an act they believe is immoral.

Where establishment is concerned, things can be equally tricky. When courts evaluate the constitutionality of a law that has the effect of promoting or funding the work of a religious institution, they ask whether it has a legitimate secular purpose or in effect serves as an endorsement of religion. Thus when a state uses government funds to pay the salaries of teachers at religious schools or requires school prayer or mandates the teaching of creationism, it violates the establishment clause. But when a state merely releases public school students early so that they can receive private religious instruction or gives tuition vouchers to parents who then can use them at any private school, including a religious school, the state has stayed within permissible bounds—it is not "endorsing" a specific church or religion.

The establishment and free exercise clauses, therefore, are *general* but not *absolute* principles of government. We apply them to our society's laws wherever possible, but we can and should make exceptions when these exceptions are necessary to promote the common good of all Americans. We might say the same for the "separation of church and state." While generally it is important to ensure that our religion stays distinct from our politics, we don't want to be so fixated on keeping our faith out of the public square that our politics loses its very soul.

A Place for Faith

The modern world constantly puts forth new challenges to the church-state distinction. What about using public funds to pay for holiday displays in public spaces? Is that a violation of the Establishment Clause? And what happens if a voter's or an officeholder's religious faith teaches that abortion or war or same-sex marriage is morally wrong? Should the person use the democratic process to make these things illegal for everyone? Questions like these now dominate the religion and politics debate in modern America, and they are the source of unprecedented conflict.

An important but often overlooked factor in addressing these questions is the distinction between *faith* and *religion*. We often use these terms interchangeably, but in reality there is a subtle and important difference, and it's most simply expressed like this: nearly everyone has faith, but not everyone has religion. This is because "faith" has a legitimate purpose outside the religious arena. We don't need to be part of any particular faith tradition, for instance, to be faithful to our spouses or to put our families first. Faith is a powerful force that drives our human action. The reason that we get out of bed in the morning, that we go to work, that we try to make the world a better place is because we have faith that these things matter—we believe in them, both in our own lives and the lives of others. Another way of speaking about faith is to speak about our *values*.

While it's true that many people's values are informed by established churches, many others have deep-seated values that come from their own individual sense of the spirit or ethics. Religion, in the context of American pluralism, is not so much faith itself as a community of faith. It's a group of people who share a common faith and common values, particularly in something supernatural or unseen. And religion tends to bring with it a set of shared rituals, traditions, and rules that distinguishes it from what is popularly called "spirituality."

Religion guides faith, and faith can guide religion, but where politics is concerned, we must be especially vigilant in remembering the distinction between the two. That's because whereas faith (really, our values) holds a very important place in the political sphere, religion should be kept out of it to the greatest possible extent. When America's founders established the world's first modern democracy, they did so because they had *faith* that government worked best when it was created by and for the people. But they were also careful to leave their *religion* at the door. This is why the Constitution makes no mention of God, the Bible, or Jesus Christ, despite the fact that all who wrote it were Christians.

A common source of confusion faced by many people of faith comes when trying to distinguish between religious principles unique to particular faith traditions (like sacraments, doctrines, and prayers) and social values that cut across religious and nonreligious traditions. Take murder, for instance. As Catholics, we believe that is wrong to take human life except in extreme cases: to defend our own life or another's. But we don't believe that murder should be illegal just for Catholics; we believe that this moral principle should apply to all human beings. This is not merely a theological stance but a philosophical standard that arises from the centuries-old tradition called *natural law*.

Natural law is a branch of moral theology that derives ethical principles from a rational understanding of nature. It trusts in part in the capacity of human reason to discern what is right by observing the state of the natural world. It's often represented as "*is* to *ought*," as in "what *is*, *ought* to be." It is also represented as the ability to distinguish between the way things are—such as the miserable conditions workers faced during the Industrial Revolution—and the way they ought to be, such as making sure these workers receive just and fair treatment. Because Catholics believe that God has created each and every human person in His image, we therefore believe it is incumbent on all of us to preserve human life. We might say the same for our environment: God created the earth and saw that it was good; therefore, we have a responsibility to keep it that way. Natural law has an important place in our own nation's political history: the signers of the Declaration of Independence believed that human beings are "are endowed by their Creator with certain unalienable Rights" and "that among these are Life, Liberty and the pursuit of Happiness." The entire idea of American freedom hinges on our belief that human beings, by their very nature, *ought* to be free.

The Importance of Compromise

Murder is a clear example of a case in which an element of Catholic teaching happens to be shared by the vast majority of Americans. But what about issues on which many of our fellow citizens differ, like abortion or stem cell research or evolution? The culture warriors have worked to convince us that it's all or nothing: either we take a stubborn, hard-nosed approach, or we leave our values out of politics altogether. But for most Americans, neither of these options leaves us feeling true to our beliefs. In order to have a political conversation that's rooted in both values and cooperation, we must work to find common ground and talk with one another—even people with whom we don't see eye to eye. This kind of dialogue allows people of differing opinions to *compromise*, that is, to overcome our divisions and find ways to make progress while respecting each other's values.

The culture warriors have worked hard to convince us that compromise equates to theological or ideological surrender. The argument goes something like this: if we believe that our deeply held convictions are right and true, accepting anything less of these convictions in our political action would call seriously into question the quality of our beliefs and our commitment to them. In short, culture warriors want us to believe that political compromise is evidence of lack of faith and that working to find common ground with those who don't share our views will somehow poison our own values.

In reality, it's exactly the opposite. Politics, in a democratic society like ours, is often referred to as the "art of compromise." This does not mean that we must compromise on our own values to have a functioning democracy. But it does mean that we must be prepared to seek compromise on how these values are reflected in public policy. Again, compromise is not the same as abandoning our values or ceasing to try to see them reflected in public life. Rather, it's usually the only way to get things done. And it's not an indicator of our lack of faith; on the contrary, it's evidence that our values are strong.

As we explored in Chapter One, we need to remember that there are many areas of life that are essential to the common good that fall outside the realm of government. Civil society, through which individuals can act together as part of nongovernmental organizations like labor unions and churches, does much to promote the common good as well. And decisions about how to spend our money, what to watch on TV, or what kinds of values to instill in our children will always rest with individuals and communities. When dealing with issues like these, it is all the more important to engage in dialogue and persuade our neighbors to make personal decisions that benefit the common good.

Where public policy is concerned, compromise holds an important place in our nation's political history. In fact, the very makeup of Congress owes itself to a famous compromise. When drafting the Constitution, the founders reached an impasse over the composition of our national legislative body. States with fewer residents wanted a fixed number of representatives per state, while more densely populated states wanted representation based on the number of residents. The solution was to allow for both: a Senate made up of two representatives from each state and a House of Representatives made up of a number of delegates determined by each state's population. The solution is known to this day as the Great Compromise, and it is regarded as an important step forward for the Constitution's framers.

Through the years, compromise has been used to achieve accord on a number of important issues. During the 1980s, Republican President Ronald Reagan worked with Democratic Speaker of the House Tip O'Neill to find compromise on much-needed reforms to save Social Security. The deal they reached allowed each side to get something it wanted: Republicans were able to raise the minimum retirement age, and Democrats succeeded in taxing Social Security benefits. Each side gave a little and got a little, and all of us were better off in the end.

The effects of lack of compromise can be devastating. Despite the fact that many Americans opposed President Bush's stated justifications for the invasion of Iraq and believed that diplomacy and negotiation could have resolved our differences peacefully, the war's supporters chose to force their policies through with little regard for the opposition's views. The result: an unpopular and seemingly endless conflict that has claimed thousands of lives and created a refugee crisis of unprecedented proportions. In recent years, our leaders have chosen similarly uncompromising paths regarding the treatment of prisoners and civil liberties, all with the result of diminishing American freedom and our nation's standing in the world, and contributing to a growing sense of political hopelessness among the American people.

Church and State in the Catholic Tradition

Most Catholics recognize intuitively the need to make a distinction between the role of the Church and the role of government. This tradition dates back to the very beginnings of our church. "Render therefore unto Caesar the things which are Caesar's," Jesus reminded the Pharisees, "and unto God the things that are God's" (Matthew 22:21). Some four hundred years later, Saint Augustine would distinguish between the natural "City of Man" and the supernatural "City of God," a theme that persists in Christian theology to this day. And writing in the Middle Ages, Saint Thomas Aquinas observed an important difference between human law (the law established by governments and societies) and the laws of God and nature. Human law *could* be informed by morality, he reasoned. But we do not aspire to draft all of these beliefs into civil law—first, because such laws would generally not be followed, and second, because our fellow citizens do not always widely share our beliefs. So while we're called as Catholics to follow higher laws of morality (such as abstaining from premarital sex and avoiding artificial contraception), instead of trying to legislate this morality, Catholics and the Church seek to convince the culture and society of their moral and social value. Because human society is by nature imperfect,

Aquinas believed, human laws will not always reflect our social ideals.

Aquinas understood that as Catholics, we don't want to use the political system to force, or *coerce*, others to live by our faith and follow our ethical codes. We believe instead that the role of the Church and of individual Catholics is to work to *persuade* others, to help, in the words of Pope Benedict XVI, to "shape their reason" and encourage them to live up to a higher moral standard. While we *can* use law to promote common good values in the public sphere, we have to remember that law is one tool among many. Our primary goal as politically engaged faithful citizens is not—in and of itself—to pass laws that mirror our values. Rather, we endeavor to build a society in which human dignity and the common good stand at the forefront of our social and cultural priorities. In many cases, the change we seek is most appropriately accomplished through other nonlegal means—through, for example, our popular culture and the ways in which we live our personal lives. "Catholic social doctrine," Pope Benedict XVI would write many centuries after Aquinas in his encyclical *Deus Caritas Est*, "has no intention of giving the Church power over the State. Even less is it an attempt to impose on those who do not share the faith ways of thinking and modes of conduct proper to faith. Its aim is simply to help purify reason and to contribute, here and now, to the acknowledgment and attainment of what is just." Even when we accept political compromise, we can continue to work to instill society and culture with common good values through the art of persuasion.

For Catholics, the modern age heralded a new era in the history of church-state relations. Prior to the eighteenth century, "secular" government in Europe and the Western world was still viewed as an extension of celestial authority: kings and queens derived their power from God as part of a "great chain of being" connecting all of society to the divine. But during the Enlightenment, when elements of Western society started to look to human reason for answers, things started to change. Instead of rule by the monarchy, rule by the people became the norm. And with democracy came *pluralism*: the belief that government and society should accommodate different cultures, political points of view, and religious traditions.

Concerned that the new world order would challenge its spiritual authority, the Church reacted to this turn of events rather strongly for a time. Pope Pius IX's 1864 *Syllabus of Errors*, for example, challenged the modern notion that "the Church ought to be separated from the State, and the State from the Church." But Catholic leaders would ultimately come to understand separation as a positive development by affirming government's responsibility to protect religious liberty in the Church's famous 1965 *Dignitatis Humanae* document—the Doctrine on Religious Freedom. Later, both Pope John Paul II and Pope Benedict XVI would speak of the "rightful autonomy" of politics from religion but remind Catholics of the importance of applying morality to public life.

Nevertheless, for much of our history in America, we Catholics have often found ourselves struggling to fit in. At the turn of the twentieth century, U.S. cities were filled with Catholic immigrants who wanted desperately to assimilate into the rest of society and at the same time feel free to practice their religion. But the Catholic Church's strong central institution and strict body of doctrines caused many non-Catholics to eye us suspiciously. Things came to a head in 1960 when John F. Kennedy found himself a serious contender to become the first Catholic president in U.S. history. Many Americans worried that Kennedy, as president, would act as the pope's puppet. In a speech in Houston, the future president famously laid these fears to rest: "I do not speak for my church on public matters," he said, "and the church does not speak for me." With these words, a new era of American Catholicism was born.

Some have argued that Kennedy went too far in separating the tenets of his faith from the work he would do as president. But we have to keep in mind the context of his decision:

only a few decades earlier, Catholics in America suffered terrible discrimination, having routinely been treated as second-class citizens (Catholic immigrants from Ireland in the 1800s were infamously greeted with "help wanted" signs bearing the acronym INNA—for "Irish Need Not Apply"). Now one of them was poised to take the highest office in the land. Kennedy knew he had no chance of becoming president unless he could convince Americans that his religion would not prevent him from faithfully executing his duty to "preserve, protect, and defend the Constitution."

Kennedy saw that controversy over his religious faith was interfering with the real moral issues at stake in the election, which included, as he put it, "the hungry children I saw in West Virginia, the old people who cannot pay their doctor bills, the families forced to give up their farms—an America with too many slums, with too few schools, and too late to the moon and outer space." He had vowed to keep his religion out of politics, but his faith and values—that society works best when we all work together—would continue to inspire his public service until the day he died.

By coincidence, another Catholic would capture the public imagination in 1960 for his own work reconciling Catholic teaching with public life in America. That year, the Jesuit theologian John Courtney Murray made headlines (including the cover of *Time*) for his book *We Hold These Truths: Catholic Reflections on the American Proposition*, which argued that the Constitution's establishment and free exercise clauses were in fact theological as well as political doctrines. While Catholics believe that all humanity can find salvation through the Church, Murray argued, we also believe that we should not try to use the democratic political system to bring the message of our religion to the world. As a matter of principle, and to keep secular authorities from co-opting our faith, the Catholic Church does not desire to be the established religion of any secular government. In the same vein, according to Murray, our church's regard for human liberty is the basis of our belief in free exercise. True faith cannot be obtained by coercion of conscience; and no power, Catholics believe, has the rightful authority to impose religion on any human being.

Where the politically active Catholic is concerned, Murray follows Aquinas's distinction between *articles of faith* and *articles of peace*. Articles of faith are the tenets of religion—the beliefs, rituals, and practices that comprise any faith tradition. Articles of peace, by contrast, are the duty of the state, whose primary role is to maintain order. The Church's mandate to go to Mass is an article of faith: we feel comfortable enforcing it in our own community but would never dream of writing it into secular law. The speed limit on your street, on the other hand, is an article of peace, necessary to maintain the safety of motorists and pedestrians but certainly not something we would expect to find in a papal encyclical.

What Kennedy and Murray had discovered, in their own ways and for their own reasons, was that Catholicism and democracy did not have to be opposing forces. One's Catholicism need not interfere with one's ability to perform one's duties in a pluralist society, and one's public duties need not interfere with one's Catholicism.

Political Compromise and the Culture of Life

As clear as the distinctions between religion and politics were to Kennedy and Murray, we need to keep in mind that our Catholic community's understanding of church and state is constantly developing in response to new ideas, new technologies, and new historical realities. Thirteen years after these men set the tone for the modern understanding of Catholicism and politics, the U.S. Supreme Court issued its landmark *Roe v. Wade* decision, effectively legalizing abortion in the United States. This move touched off a long and controversial chain of events with far-reaching repercussions for our Catholic community.

The central question for our church concerned the Catholic officeholder's moral duty with regard to ending and preventing abortion. Those who may have personally opposed abortion but were not willing to work toward making it illegal—or more commonly, those who represented constituents who insisted on keeping abortion legal—found themselves in a difficult position after *Roe* v. *Wade*. Many struggled to find a way to reconcile their faith with their duties as public servants. Others went so far as supporting government funding of abortion or opposing criminalization of abortion without offering other ways to deal with the problem. In most cases, these Catholics appealed to the distinction between church and state as the reason they could not impose the teachings of their faith on members of other faiths. As Catholic New York governor Mario Cuomo observed in a famous 1984 speech at Notre Dame:

> A Catholic who is elected to serve Jews and Muslims and atheists and Protestants, as well as Catholics, bears special responsibility. He or she undertakes to help create conditions under which all can live with a maximum of dignity and with a reasonable degree of freedom; where everyone who chooses may hold beliefs different from specifically Catholic ones, sometimes even contradictory to them; where the laws protect people's right to divorce, their right to use birth control devices, and even to choose abortion.

He went on:

> As Catholics, my wife and I were enjoined never to use abortion to destroy the life we created, and we never have. We thought Church doctrine was clear on this. And more than that, both of us felt it in full agreement with what our own hearts and our own consciences told us.... But not everyone in our society agrees with [us]. And those who don't—those who endorse legalized abortions—aren't a ruthless, callous alliance of anti-Christians determined to overthrow our moral standards. In many cases, the

proponents of legal abortion are the very people who have worked with Catholics to realize the goals of social justice set out by popes in encyclicals.

Cuomo, like Kennedy, was distinguishing between his religion and his responsibilities as a public official in a democratic society. He believed that while Catholic elected officials should maintain a personal opposition to abortion, they were not compelled to force this teaching on others. But his feelings were not shared by all Catholics or Church leaders, and they underscored a growing rift in our community. While ending abortion is clearly an article of faith, it is also for many Americans and for the Catholic Church an article of peace, just like our duty to oppose murder, poverty, war, and other threats to human life. We believe in addressing these issues not just because our church instructs us to do so but because they speak, in the natural law tradition, to the very value of life itself. John Cardinal O'Connor, the archbishop of New York who clashed with Cuomo over abortion on many occasions, clearly stated his opinion in 1990: in cases where Catholic elected officials insist on "advocating legislation supporting abortion or by making public funds available for abortion," he insisted, "bishops may consider excommunication the only option."

The Church released a series of statements during the reign of John Paul II clarifying the responsibility of Catholic elected officials to uphold certain teachings in office—in particular, the pope's landmark 1995 encyclical *Evangelium Vitae*, the "Gospel of Life." In 2002, Cardinal Joseph Ratzinger (who would soon become Pope Benedict XVI), head of the Vatican's Congregation for the Doctrine of the Faith, issued one of the strongest appeals to date, a document titled the *Doctrinal Note on Some Questions Regarding the Participation of Catholics in Public Life*. Intended as a message to Catholic voters and candidates, it affirmed the special importance of certain issues in modern politics, particularly abortion, stem cell research, religious freedom, economic justice, and peace. It was also careful to make clear that while officeholders are not bound to *impose* Church teachings on their constituents as part of their public duty, they are bound to be "morally coherent." And moral coherence, where abortion is concerned, means pursuing public policy to protect the unborn:

> Legislative proposals are put forward which, heedless of the consequences for the existence and future of human beings with regard to the formation of culture and social behaviour, attack the very inviolability of human life. Catholics, in this difficult situation, have the right and the duty to recall society to a deeper understanding of human life and to the responsibility of everyone in this regard. John Paul II, continuing the constant teaching of the Church, has reiterated many times that those who are directly involved in lawmaking bodies have a *"grave and clear obligation to oppose"* any law that attacks human life. For them, as for every Catholic, it is impossible to promote such laws or to vote for them.

The *Doctrinal Note* contained nothing new, really. The Vatican's intent was to restate Church teaching on the responsibilities of Catholic officeholders. But it happened to come just before Senator John Kerry became the first Catholic presidential nominee since Kennedy and since the fateful *Roe* v. *Wade* decision. In a move that cut to the very heart of the faith, political operatives on the far right called for bishops to deny Communion to those candidates who held the "wrong" positions on issues like abortion and same-sex marriage. And Kerry, who said he was personally opposed to abortion but supported keeping the practice legal, became their primary target. Writing in April 2004, Karl Keating of the lay group Catholic Answers labeled Kerry "precisely the kind of politician who should be denied Communion at Catholic parishes because his strong endorsement of abortion qualifies him as a 'notorious sinner.'"

Publicly, these culture warriors claimed that their goal was to hold Kerry and others accountable to essential aspects of

Catholic teaching. But most observers saw it as a thinly veiled attempt to keep the senator out of the White House. In the Catholic tradition, Communion, or the Eucharist, is considered the most important and most fundamental aspect of our religious practice, when we come into the real presence of Jesus Christ by sharing a meal of bread and wine that has been transformed into his body and blood. To prohibit a Catholic from receiving this sacrament carries the message that he or she is living publicly in a state of very grave sin. For lay members of the Catholic Church, the only punishment worse than denying Communion is excommunication, complete separation from the Church community. The culture warriors knew what they were doing: by suggesting that Kerry was a "bad" Catholic, they thought, they could convince others that he was unfit for their vote. It was a terrible misuse of faith in the political sphere and a terrible disservice to the common good. The culture warriors could have supported a pastoral or private approach with Senator Kerry and avoided a public spectacle. They could have focused on how the candidates would actually make progress on the important issues at stake in the election—like war, abortion, and poverty. Instead they went after the voters, arguing that the most important thing to consider at the polls was whether or not Kerry was in complete agreement with the teachings of his Church.

Our church leaders in Rome refused to support the notion that the Eucharist should be used as a political weapon, instead leaving the question of denial of Communion to each individual bishop. Although only a very small percentage of bishops indicated they would deny the sacrament, the issue became an unfortunate theme in the 2004 election and served only to deepen the divisions in our society and detract from the common good. It also threatened to turn the Church's sacraments into public spectacles rather than matters to be discussed between officeholders and their pastors.

Is it right for us to expect Catholic officeholders to behave in certain ways where abortion and other issues are concerned?

On one hand, as we have seen, our values, including the values of our religion, make up who we are as human beings. An officeholder who is Catholic and who holds the values instilled by the Catholic Church has a duty to act according to those values. On the other hand, that same officeholder must use his or her prudential judgment to determine how best and when to represent those standards as law in order to achieve those values. While the culture warriors were happy to quote the parts of the *Doctrinal Note* that appeared to bolster their case, they conveniently left out certain details that could have helped our nation experience a more productive political debate on abortion and other issues. Quoting the encyclical *Evangelium Vitae*, the *Note* pointed out that when "it is not possible to overturn or completely repeal a law allowing abortion which is already in force or coming up for a vote, 'an elected official, whose absolute personal opposition to procured abortion was well known, could licitly support proposals aimed at *limiting the harm* done by such a law and at lessening its negative consequences at the level of general opinion and public morality.'"

Unfortunately, abortion has become one of the most tragic examples of lack of compromise and thus real progress in U.S. politics today. Consider the way this issue typically plays out in our current political debate. One side asserts that abortion ought always to be illegal and the other that it ought always to be legal. They fight tooth and nail over this issue and have spent untold millions of dollars to make sure that each gets its own way. While both sides continue to stick to their views, year after year, nothing changes. In the end we all lose as lawmakers squabble over symbolic legislation that has no actual effect in the real world, and party surrogates badger candidates and officeholders to declare whether they are "pro-life" or "pro-choice."

A big part of the problem is that most Americans fall somewhere in between the two extremes of the abortion debate. They have serious moral concerns regarding abortion, but they are not comfortable outlawing it altogether. Nor do they think that entirely outlawing it would most effectively reduce or end abortions. Both sides should be able to put aside their differences and find a good compromise—common ground—in favor of a shared goal: to prevent and reduce abortions to the greatest possible extent. Global and U.S. data shows that providing health care and economic assistance to women and families, robust alternatives such as support for adoption and appropriate and effective sex education for young people, and a host of other policy measures have proved to reduce the abortion rate in the United States and around the world. We'll examine abortion and other pressing issues in more detail in Chapter Five, "An Agenda for the Common Good."

As a Church community, we need to understand that in addition to passing laws that tell others what they can and cannot do, we must work to change the culture by influencing hearts and minds. This is particularly the case when we talk about tackling our go-it-alone culture of materialism and excessive individualism. Where public policy is concerned, it *is* possible to reflect the values of one's faith in democratic society without forcing one's religion on others. The key is to use persuasion and compromise as tools to find common ground with others in ways that don't require sacrificing our core beliefs. For Catholics and all people of goodwill, learning how to persuade and compromise is essential to overcoming the politics of division. So is having a clear sense of the values we hold in common, as well as an understanding of the ways in which these values can be brought to bear to help us find productive solutions to the key challenges of our time. In the next chapter, we examine more closely how Catholics can engage in the world of politics, in particular through voting.

4

Voting Catholic

The 2004 presidential election witnessed an unprecedented effort to convince Catholics that it was immoral to vote for certain candidates, particularly the Democratic nominee, Catholic Senator John Kerry. Kerry claimed to be "personally opposed" to abortion but believed that the practice should remain legal—and on many occasions he had voted accordingly. How unprecedented was this 2004 Catholic outreach effort? The Republican National Committee (RNC) enlisted the help of paid Catholic field organizers to help bring its message directly to voters. From out of nowhere, blogs with names like "Catholics Against Kerry" and "Kerry Wrong for Catholics" echoed the party line. A number of groups on the far right lent their voices, with Catholic League president Bill Donohue, for example, pursuing a relentless campaign to paint Kerry's religious outreach director, an Evangelical, as anti-Catholic. And "Catholic" voting guides began popping up in churches and on car windshields after Sunday Mass, claiming that five "non-negotiable" issues trumped everything else at the voting booth.

Catholics in hotly contested swing states were bombarded with messages essentially claiming that they must either vote for Bush or go to confession. It was a morally questionable strategy, to say the least, but one that nonetheless proved tremendously effective—so much so that even the secular media came to believe the dubious idea that a religious test could indeed be applied to Catholic candidates. "The senator is aligned with his church on many social justice issues, including immigration, poverty, health care and the death penalty," the *New York Times* reported early in the campaign. "But he diverges on the *litmus* issues, like abortion and stem cell research, that animate church conservatives and many in the hierarchy [emphasis added]."

No doubt some of those who echoed this message were faithful Catholics who were acting out of a genuine desire to protect human life and dignity. A small group of Catholic bishops spoke out publicly, earning significant national media coverage all the way up to the election. But something bigger was clearly afoot. One of the best-kept secrets of the election was the unprecedented degree to which Republican outreach committees, conservative power brokers, and organizations outside the Church institution sought to convince Catholics to support the far right's political agenda. It was a low point for Catholics and the democratic process, and for the most part completely out of line with the social teachings of our church.

Many Catholics were horrified at the way their faith was misused for political gain in the 2004 election because from the earliest days of our nation, we have cherished our ability to vote in ways that promote prudent and sensible common good policies and recognize the essential connections, as well as the important distinctions, that exist among so many issues. Like other Americans, we've believed that voting is a deeply personal act, a duty and a privilege not to be taken lightly—especially when we consider the plights of the billions of people around the world who are denied the opportunity to participate in the process of government. We've also believed that however public our discussion of faith and politics should be, voting is ultimately a personal decision that must be made in good conscience between each of us and God.

By the time the dust settled, it was clear that the 2004 election would be remembered as an unfortunate time for U.S. Catholics, marked by bitter arguments that divided friends, families, and parishes. But there is a silver lining: the election raised some important and challenging questions about just what it means to be a politically engaged faithful citizen. Are some issues more important than others at the voting booth? Can Catholics vote for candidates who do not support the Church's positions on these issues? And since no party or candidate will ever fit the full spectrum of Catholic teaching, how do Catholics go about weighing which issues are most important and deciding how to vote in any given election?

Equally important, how did our community's once civil dialogue about faith and politics descend into an angry and hostile dispute, and how can we return to an open, honest, and respectful conversation about how best to represent the values of Catholicism in public life? In this chapter, we take a look at the history of the struggle over the Catholic vote and offer our own thoughts on what it means to cast our ballots in line with the teachings of our faith. There are no easy answers to any of these questions. But we sincerely hope that the ideas we present here will help restore a sense of hope and decency to our national debate on faith and politics.

Catholics and the Religious Right

The election of 2004 represented the high-water mark for the Christian right movement in America. It wasn't the first time that this movement had worked in close coordination with the Republican Party to elevate particular social issues in a national presidential election, nor was it the first time that millions of dollars were spent to turn out people of faith to vote on those issues. But the 2004 election was an extraordinary time for the political right in terms of sheer effectiveness, and for the fact that Catholic voters were incorporated into this movement as never before.

To understand the political context of 2004, we need to go back a few years—all the way back, in fact, to the 1970s. It was then that the Democratic Party made an ill-fated strategic decision to shake off its traditional alliances with faith communities and that a new movement of theological and political conservatism began to gel in Evangelical Protestant communities. In large part, this "Christian right" movement arose in response to the social and cultural excesses and changes of the 1960s. It tended toward strict biblical fundamentalism and worked to bring greater national attention to issues like homosexuality, contraception, and abortion. Most important, the movement actively sought the necessary power in Washington to see its social agenda and religious beliefs implemented in law. Its leaders were figures like Jerry Falwell, founder of the Moral Majority, and Pat Robertson, founder of the Christian Coalition, who routinely issued controversial and incendiary statements designed to stoke the fires of social backlash. It was largely through their work that the culture wars and the politics of division were born.

Although the Christian right played a large part in Ronald Reagan's 1980 election to the presidency, the movement was generally frustrated by an inability to make more than token progress in implementing its own political program (Robertson would mount an unsuccessful campaign against George H. W. Bush for the 1988 Republican presidential nomination). Instead of addressing the moral and cultural issues favored by the Christian right, those in power were instead focused on a pro–big business agenda that included cutting taxes and social programs, downsizing government, and increasing military spending. Desperate to build a bigger and more effective base, the largely Evangelical Christian right began stepping up its Catholic outreach efforts. In the 1990s, the movement participated in a series of high-profile calls for political unity between Evangelicals and Catholics, and in 1995, the Christian Coalition launched the Catholic Alliance (no relation to Catholics in Alliance), a short-lived side project designed to draft Catholics into the organization, and "speak out," in the words of its director, Ralph Reed, "against anti-Catholic bigotry."

Meanwhile, Republican strategists were grasping the fact that even a small shift in the Catholic vote could sway future elections in their favor. But despite their general opposition to abortion and same-sex marriage, many everyday Catholics were resistant to the Republican Party's take on economic issues and the role of government in a democratic society. Pope John Paul II, in addition to his strong anticommunism and his clear stance on abortion and sexual morality, had repeatedly affirmed the Church's support for social and economic justice, as well as fervent opposition to the death penalty—all issues that flew in the face of the party's agenda. Operatives realized that to convince Catholics to join the movement, they needed to diminish the importance of these social justice teachings and build a case that the candidates' stated positions on the *legality* of abortion and same-sex marriage were the only important considerations for Catholic voters. In effect, they had to reduce the breadth of Catholic teaching to those issues that served the far right's political program.

Political strategists went to work crafting an organizing plan. Chief among these efforts was a 1998 study by the conservative Catholic magazine *Crisis*, which pointed to a specific group of churchgoing Catholics as a prime prospect for new organizing. Though it claimed to be an objective look at Catholic voting patterns, the study reads like a road map for Republican outreach efforts, proclaiming hopefully that "religiously active Catholics are at last aligning politically with born-again, evangelical Christians" and complaining that "most Catholics favor some degree of government regulation in the economic sphere."

Crisis editor Deal Hudson, who in 1994 had been forced from his post at Fordham University in the wake of a sex scandal, successfully pitched his plan to capture the Catholic vote to Republican strategists, and Bush adviser Karl Rove invited him to lead the campaign's Catholic outreach efforts. The RNC went on to pour millions of dollars into a "Catholic task force" to win over the hearts and minds of U.S. Catholics during the 2000 election campaign, an endeavor that bore fruit in heavily Catholic states like Florida. Bush's first term saw the renewal of the RNC's Catholic outreach efforts for the 2002 midterm elections. That year, USA Today reported that in preparation for the next elections, "conservative Catholics are being given unprecedented access to the White House and policy decisions."

Then, in the spring of 2004, the bishops of a handful of U.S. Roman Catholic dioceses announced that they would withhold Communion from Catholic politicians whose votes were inconsistent with Church teaching on abortion. For supporters of an unpopular president looking to keep the White House for another term, the timing of this move could not have been more convenient. Senator John Kerry was running as the first Catholic nominee for president since John F. Kennedy, and the election was shaping up to be one of the closest and most important in history. Indeed, a couple of conservative bishops went as far as to suggest that even pulling the lever for Kerry was sinful. "If you vote this way, are you cooperating in evil?" Archbishop Charles Chaput of Denver told the New York Times a few weeks before the election. "And if you know you are cooperating in evil, should you go to confession? The answer is yes." Though Chaput's comments represented a minority opinion even among his fellow bishops, the rap on Kerry's knuckles became welcome fodder for a conflict-hungry news media. Less well-funded efforts to promote the Catholic social justice tradition—such as the Catholic Voting Project (which would later become Chris's organization, Catholics United) and Pax Christi's "Life Does Not End at Birth" campaign—received much less attention in the press. Media coverage of the senator's "Catholic problem" left many

Americans with the impression that the Catholic Church was backing Bush in 2004 and that Kerry's pro-choice stance made him completely unfit for the Catholic vote. "Kerry's support for abortion rights and civil unions for gay couples raises the ire of church leaders," the Associated Press wrote in August 2004, "while Bush, a Methodist, is more in line with Catholic teaching on those issues."

There was only one problem: despite any misgivings they may have had about some of Kerry's political views, most of the leaders of the U.S. Catholic Church took a much more measured approach to the election. While they called for action to protect marriage and the unborn, they also insisted that avoiding war, ending poverty, and improving health care and education were essential moral concerns for Catholic voters to consider and not irrelevant to the larger concerns of abortion and failing marriages. And only a small number publicly supported denying Communion to Catholic candidates or imposing "litmus tests" on Catholics voters. Whatever popular notion existed that Catholics could not, according to the laws of their church, vote in good conscience for candidates of either major political party was a total fabrication, perpetrated by people with their own political axes to grind. Speaking about denying Communion in April 2004, Bishop Wilton Gregory, then president of the United States Conference of Catholic Bishops, told the Catholic News Service that "in the nature of the church, the imposition of sanctions is always the final response, not the first response, nor the second, nor maybe even the 10th." In October, retired Archbishop John Quinn of San Francisco said in a homily that it is not "prudent for bishops to tell the Catholic people which among several candidates they should vote for."

Indeed, Cardinal Joseph Ratzinger (who one year later would become Pope Benedict XVI) went as far as to say that it *could* be acceptable for Catholics to vote for candidates with the "wrong" positions on abortion, as long as they weren't voting *because* of those positions and as long as they were voting because other grave moral reasons existed.

The "Communion controversy," which would not be completely resolved in time for the 2008 presidential election, represented a low point for U.S. Catholics. It gave many Americans the impression that the Church was taking sides in partisan politics, and by turning attention away from other important issues, like war, poverty, and the environment, greatly diminished the fullness of Catholic social teaching in the public sphere. It also gave the very false impression that Catholic voters were little more than a collection of mindless robots who, instead of taking the time to think and discern how best to vote to achieve their values, were being bullied into following a simple and mechanical formula.

Demanding that candidates, officeholders, and voters follow a political blueprint creates the appearance that the Church's most important sacrament should be used as a political weapon. It also deprives Catholics of the ability to use *prudence* in applying the principles of our faith to political action. One way it does this is by buying in to the false idea that all our leaders have to do in order to support the unborn is to state whether they *think* abortion should be illegal, when we really should be more concerned about what our leaders will *do* to promote and defend human life. Indeed, in 2004, many Catholics felt that the key to ending abortion was to lessen the burden many families feel trying to raise children today—for instance, to expand health care and job protections or provide child care and other services to young children. They understood that a society could not reflect a true culture of life if it didn't do everything it could do to provide support for pregnant women. But the culture warriors told us that all we were allowed to do was vote for the candidates who claimed to oppose legal abortion, regardless of whether we felt those candidates would or could actually do anything to follow through on their beliefs. In essence, the Communion ban forced Catholic candidates and voters to make a terrible decision: either choose sides in the politics of division or exclude ourselves from full participation in our church.

Theology and the Politics of Division

Even before the Communion controversy surfaced in 2004, well-funded Republican surrogates were preparing an unprecedented push to scare Catholics into supporting Bush's reelection bid. In the summer of 2004, a San Diego–based group called Catholic Answers released the *Voter's Guide for Serious Catholics*, a twelve-page booklet that claimed that five "nonnegotiable" issues trumped the Church's cherished social justice teachings at the polls: abortion, same-sex marriage, euthanasia, human cloning, and stem cell research—all issues that worked in favor of Bush (mostly because of his stated opposition to them rather than any policies he would ultimately pursue) and against Kerry. The guide's official release was timed to coincide with the Republican National Convention in August and September of that year and reached millions of Catholics through widespread grassroots distribution and full-page ads in major national papers. Despite our own movement's best efforts to present a full accounting of Catholic teaching as it related to the election, the Catholic Answers message captured the media's attention through election day, leaving many Catholics with a skewed impression of their church's social teachings.

Catholic Answers, which purports to be nonpartisan, was a well-respected organization dedicated to helping Catholics understand and defend the teachings of their faith. But the *Voter's Guide for Serious Catholics* took the organization in a whole new direction, in the process seriously undermining its reputation for presenting an accurate and unbiased account of the teachings of our church. Instead of promoting existing Church doctrines, Catholic Answers began inventing new ones, and many people viewed the *Voter's Guide* as a thinly veiled attempt to coerce faithful Catholics into supporting the president's reelection bid.

The *Voter's Guide for Serious Catholics* was a theological disaster. It argued essentially that voting for a candidate made the
voter morally responsible for everything that candidate would do
in office. Since the five issues in question were never morally
acceptable for any reason, the guide claimed, it was never
morally acceptable to vote for candidates who did not hold
the Catholic position on these issues. The key to this argument
is the word *never*. It doesn't matter, the *Voter's Guide* argues, if
you feel that the candidate is lying to you or making promises
he or she can't keep, or even if you feel that the candidate who
doesn't think abortion should be illegal will do more in the end
to lower the abortion rate and build a culture of life. If you believe
what the *Voter's Guide* says, you are obligated to follow a Catholic
voting formula. Your own judgment about how best to realize the
values of our faith is completely irrelevant.

Despite its claims to authenticity, the *Voter's Guide* received
little, if any, support from the institutional Church. The United
States Conference of Catholic Bishops had actually produced its
own statement on civic engagement, as it does ahead of every
presidential election. Called *Faithful Citizenship: A Catholic Call
to Political Responsibility*, it emphasized the special and fundamental importance of life issues and also listed some fifty "moral
priorities for public life," grounded in the very heart of Catholic
teaching—everything from health care and the war in Iraq
to the death penalty and the environment. What's more, the
bishops repeatedly stated that *Faithful Citizenship* was the only
national Catholic voter information approved for use in Catholic
churches. But this did little to stop Catholic Answers in its quest
to reelect President Bush.

Perhaps the most significant repudiation of the Catholic
Answers voting theology came from the Vatican itself. In June
2004, Cardinal Ratzinger of the Congregation of the Doctrine for
the Faith wrote to the USCCB to restate the need for Catholic
officeholders to abide by Church teachings and not vote for

"intrinsically unjust" laws, such as those that support abortion or euthanasia. The letter includes the following footnote:

> A Catholic would be guilty of formal cooperation in evil, and so unworthy to present himself for Holy Communion, if he were to deliberately vote for a candidate precisely because of the candidate's permissive stand on abortion and/or euthanasia. When a Catholic does not share a candidate's stand in favour of abortion and/or euthanasia, but votes for that candidate for other reasons, it is considered remote material cooperation, which can be permitted in the presence of proportionate reasons.

At the risk of getting too heady, let's take a quick look at the theology behind Cardinal Ratzinger's statement. As faithful Catholics, we are called to do good and avoid evil. But sometimes in the process of doing good, we have to accept that our actions may have the side effect of cooperating with an evil action. In modern-day society, it's almost impossible to live our lives without a few bad side effects. Take our cars, for example. Every time we drive, we create pollution, which ultimately threatens the health of other humans. But often our cars are essential to our being productive and contributing members of society. The harm to others done by our pollution is indeed an evil, but it's one we tolerate for the greater good of being able to get to work. We understand that the act of driving is not the same as putting poison in someone's drink.

To distinguish between cooperation in evil for which we are and are not morally responsible, Catholic theology uses the terms *formal* and *material*. *Formal cooperation* is when we intend to do evil or when we intend to participate in an evil act. *Material cooperation*, by contrast, is when our good action has other evil consequences. Performing an abortion or driving someone to an abortion clinic to have one would be a clear example of formal cooperation in evil. But voting for a candidate who does not believe abortion should be illegal would constitute only material cooperation.

The Church does teach that there are certain actions that are never morally acceptable. These "intrinsic evils" ("non-negotiable issues" in Catholic Answers lingo) include abortion and euthanasia, and our *formal* participation in them is always wrong, no matter what the reason. In the vast majority of cases, though, we must understand the circumstance and the intent of a person's action in order to determine whether the action is right or wrong. Contrary to what the *Voter's Guide for Serious Catholics* would have us believe, the act of casting a vote (even for a candidate who supports an intrinsically evil act) cannot itself be considered intrinsically evil, precisely because we always have to consider the voter's intent. The bottom line, as Cardinal Ratzinger was reminding us, is that no one can judge whether we voted correctly without first understanding *why* we voted the way we did.

There are many cases in Catholic moral theology in which it's possible for one action to be wrong and an identical action to be right if the two actions are performed in different situations with different intent. Consider the following hypothetical situation: Chris is standing around minding his own business, and Alexia comes along and pushes him to the ground, causing him to break his arm. Was Alexia right or wrong in her action? The answer might seem obvious, but what if Chris was actually standing in the middle of the street and Alexia was pushing him out of the way of a fast-approaching bus? In this way, a broken arm can be either a horrible injustice or a small price to pay in accomplishing the much greater good of saving someone's life. It all depends on circumstances and intent. The same goes for the taking of human life. Person A pulls out a gun and shoots person B. If person A is a bank robber and person B is the teller, it's a very different story than if person A is a police officer and person B is a terrorist about to detonate a bomb.

So why should things be any different when it comes to the moral action of pulling a lever in the voting booth? Cardinal

Ratzinger's point is that it shouldn't: we can't judge whether a voter was right or wrong unless we understand the circumstances of the vote and the voter's intent in voting the way he or she did. Let's consider two candidates, X and Y. Candidate X says he believes abortion should not be made illegal but supports working to prevent abortions by expanding health coverage for children and families, funding for child care and Head Start programs, and expanding other assistance for mothers and for working families. Candidate Y says he believes abortion should be illegal but wants to cut funding for health care and economic assistance to citizens in need. If Chris votes for candidate X *because of* candidate X's position on abortion—because Chris shares the candidate's belief that abortion is something our society should tolerate—he should really consider a visit to the confession booth. But if Chris votes for candidate X for other reasons—for instance, because he believes that the candidate's policies will ultimately do more to help the unborn than anti-abortion candidate Y—he *can* be justified in his actions. What if he votes for candidate Y? Again, it depends *why*. If it's because he shares the candidate's belief that people should just look after themselves and neglect our responsibility to safeguard the welfare of our fellow human beings, Chris would also be in great need of a confessor.

Now, this *doesn't* mean that we should feel warranted in voting for whomever we choose for whatever reasons we deem appropriate. We'd all agree, for instance, that a candidate's physical looks are not an acceptable justification for voting for one over another, and as Cardinal Ratzinger reminded the USCCB in his memo, the reasons for justifying a vote for candidate X must be *proportionate*. What constitutes a proportionate reason? Because our church does not provide us with a list, we should consider this a topic for open and productive dialogue within our community. But the point is that it's impossible to judge someone's vote on the basis of the vote alone. We have to know *why* a person voted as he or she did and what the person was hoping to achieve, and this means we have to engage in dialogue with the person. "The memo was certainly not intended to clear the way for Catholics to vote for candidates who are in favor of laws permitting abortion or euthanasia," the undersecretary of the Congregation for the Doctrine of the Faith, Father Augustine Di Noia, told the Catholic News Service in September 2004, "but rather to clarify that the simple act of voting for such candidates might not per se justify one's exclusion from Holy Communion."

Voting for the Common Good

Our own movement vowed never again to let a partisan or non-Catholic organization mislead Catholics for political gain. In 2006, Catholics in Alliance produced its own guide, called *Voting for the Common Good: A Practical Guide for Conscientious Catholics.* Unlike the Catholic Answers guide, *Voting for the Common Good* insisted that our church institution was the best source of information for Catholic voters. At every possible turn, Alexia and her staff encouraged voters to look to the USCCB's *Faithful Citizenship* document, as well as the Vatican's *Compendium of the Social Doctrine of the Church.* The Catholics in Alliance guide focused on the entirety of the Catholic social tradition and urged Catholics to inform their conscience about the Church's teaching and to use common sense—*prudential judgment,* as our tradition calls it—to determine how best to respect Catholic values at the voting booth.

Voting for the Common Good became an instant success, so much so that Alexia's mailing operation could scarcely keep up with the demand. Orders poured in from around the country, from parish priests, campus ministry offices, and everyday Catholics who had hungered for this message based on Catholic social teaching. In all, Catholics in Alliance distributed about half a million copies in the six weeks prior to the election and reached countless more people through a downloadable version and through media coverage. People loved the simplicity, authenticity, and orthodoxy of the guide, which encouraged the faithful to consider three principles with regard to voting: *inform your conscience* on Church teaching and the candidates' positions, *use prudence* when deciding how to apply Catholic values to voting, and *vote for the common good* by focusing on what's best for everyone, especially the poor and vulnerable.

It's important to note that we do not claim that *Voting for the Common Good* is an official Catholic Church "voting guide" or statement. It is produced by a lay Catholic organization and is intended as a tool for lay Catholics to use to become more familiar with Catholic social teaching and the Catholic ethics of voting.

Inform Your Conscience

The Catholic tradition teaches that our conscience is essential to making any moral decision, including voting. Our conscience helps us know right from wrong, but in order to vote according to our conscience, we must *inform* it, by learning about the Church's positions on important issues. One of the best sources of this information is the USCCB's *Faithful Citizenship* document.

Next, research the candidates' positions on these issues by visiting their Web sites, reading media coverage about their campaigns, and talking to your friends and family. It's important to look at a candidate's actions—particularly how he or she has acted on issues in the past, in addition to what he or she is saying about the issue today—in order to understand how he or she may act in the future.

Use Prudence

While an informed conscience is essential for knowing right from wrong, actually doing the right thing requires the virtue of prudence. Prudence is the moral wisdom required to apply principles to an imperfect world and unforeseeable circumstances. It is like a "moral common sense," and it requires us to ask the practical question "Which candidate will actually deliver more tangible progress to promote human dignity and achieve the common good?"

As the *Catechism of the Catholic Church* explains, "It is prudence that immediately guides the judgment of conscience.... With the help of this virtue we apply moral principles to particular cases without error and overcome doubts about the good to achieve and the evil to avoid." Through prudence, we apply the law written in our hearts to real-world circumstances.

Prudence is especially important when deciding how to vote. Seldom does a single candidate or party offer a consistently Catholic set of positions. For example, a candidate may not entirely share the Church's principles on an issue but still do much through his or her actions to promote the Catholic social tradition. The Church's social teaching is clear, but many times Catholics disagree on the best way to achieve justice and dignity in the world.

We seldom, if ever, have the opportunity to vote for a candidate with the right positions on all the issues important to Catholics. In order to maximize the good our vote achieves, Catholics must thoughtfully and prayerfully consider and debate what is most pressing and possible in our time. It is OK for us to disagree about who and what to vote for, as long as our decisions are made with conscience informed by our church's teachings, and made prudently.

Vote for the Common Good

As politically active Catholics, our primary responsibility is to the common good. The common good provides for the health, welfare, and dignity of all people and promotes the best interests of everyone, not just the few. It ensures that we truly build the essential conditions for a culture of life. It also focuses on helping those who need it most: the poor and vulnerable. When we vote for the common good, we vote to build a society in which all have the freedom and opportunity to reach their full human potential.

Ultimately, only the individual voter can answer the question of which candidates will have the most positive effect on human dignity and the common good.

Forming Consciences for Faithful Citizenship

In 2007, as it does every four years, the United States Conference of Catholic Bishops issued a revision of the *Faithful Citizenship* document. Called *Forming Consciences for Faithful Citizenship*, it was the first since the controversies of the 2004 election. It was also the first time in history that the entire Conference, rather than a select committee, had voted to approve a *Faithful Citizenship* release. The document helps clarify some points of confusion that had arisen in the Catholic community in the intervening years and also addresses some new moral challenges. It makes clear that abortion and other direct threats to human life are preeminent concerns and never acceptable. And it points to other unacceptable threats to human life, like genocide, torture, and the targeting of noncombatants in war or terrorism. It also states unequivocally the bishops' disapproval of the sort of litmus test approach to voting that had driven Catholic Answers and the Republicans' 2004 campaign. "A Catholic cannot vote for a candidate who takes a position in favor of an intrinsic evil, such as abortion or racism, if the voter's *intent* is to support that position," the bishops write. "At the same time, a voter should not use a candidate's opposition to an intrinsic evil to justify indifference or inattentiveness to other important moral issues involving human life and dignity [emphasis added]."

The bishops stress the fact that their document does not tell Catholics whom to vote for or against. Rather, they present it as a "moral framework" intended to help Catholics make decisions with a conscience formed by the fullness of the Catholic faith, applying the Catholic principle of prudence, and analyzing choices in light of the Catholic social tradition. In deference to the need for Catholic voters to seek workable approaches to the concerns of the modern world, and in direct repudiation of the message of the *Voter's Guide for Serious Catholics*, the bishops note that "prudence shapes and informs our ability to deliberate over available alternatives, to determine what is most fitting to a specific context, and to act decisively."

Emphasizing the dignity of the human person as the core principle of Catholic teaching, the bishops assert the importance of bringing this principle into the public square. Citizens' responsibility to promote the common good through political participation flows from this central concern for human dignity and the requirement to love our neighbor. What exactly is the goal of "faithful citizenship" on the part of Catholic voters? According to the bishops, it is to "contribute to greater justice and peace for all people" and to "help build a better world."

Forming Consciences for Faithful Citizenship offers more specific policy priorities through the lens of Catholic teaching. These issues are organized into the categories of "human life," "family life," "social justice," and "global solidarity." Issues from health care to the economy, abortion to war, poverty to the environment, education to immigration are addressed through the lens of the Catholic social tradition as well. The full text of the document, as well as a condensed parish bulletin insert, is available for use in churches or community events at http://www.faithfulcitizenship.org.

In the next chapter, "An Agenda for the Common Good," we take a deeper look at how the Catholic social tradition and concern for the common good can be brought to bear on the pressing moral concerns of our day.

5

An Agenda for the Common Good

In this book, we attempt to answer a central question: how can we transcend the politics of division and begin to reclaim our nation's commitment to the common good? In answering this question, we've talked about the need for dialogue, and the importance of engaging our differences by paying more attention to shared values and political commonalities. We've looked at the relationship between faith—specifically, our Catholic faith—and a free and democratic society like that of the United States. And we've seen how living out our faith in the public square calls us to shape our consciences in light of the Church's teachings, to apply the "moral common sense" of prudence, and to cast our votes with an eye toward real results.

The politics of division is so deeply ingrained in our collective national consciousness that we can easily spend all of our time trying to undo the misconceptions it has created. But an essential component of overcoming this division is to move beyond the culture war and focus more on the kind of society we *should* have and less on the kind we *shouldn't*. We can accomplish this by making good personal choices and electing good leaders. We also have to ask, how can we, as Catholic citizens, construct and support public policies that address the moral concerns that are important to our faith and the common good?

As with voting, there is no one right way to answer this question, and it's seldom possible to point to a single feasible and faithful Catholic political agenda where any given issue is concerned. There are just too many variables to account for. How, for instance, do we balance the need for social order with the central democratic principle of freedom? How do we square the Catholic belief in economic justice for all with the American notion of free-market capitalism? How do we weigh our own moral convictions against the multitude of other interests at play in the political arena? Most important of all, how do we discover a sense of what is *possible* and, rather than getting stuck in the politics of division, apply the arts of persuasion and compromise to promote the common good and human dignity effectively?

It's because of questions like these that the leaders of the Catholic Church do not claim to speak with absolute authority on matters of government and public policy. Although this may come as a surprise to some, it makes sense when we consider the rightful distinction between church and state, between religion and politics, as well as the need never to regard one as a substitute for the other. "A just society must be the achievement of politics, not of the Church," writes Pope Benedict XVI in his encyclical *Deus Caritas Est.* Instead, the Church's role is to provide the proper moral guidance and formation of conscience to help us make the right political decisions. The Church is here "to contribute to the purification of reason and to the reawakening of those moral forces without which just structures are neither established nor prove effective in the long run," the pope reminds us. "The direct duty to work for a just ordering of society, on the other hand, is proper to the lay faithful."

While our church indeed speaks with authority on many political *issues*, it recognizes that determining the most effective political *solutions* is often a different matter. Democracy is about forging solutions out of a diversity of positions, and each of us can and should engage in dialogue with others, identify common ground, and feel free to disagree respectfully on matters of policy.

The United States Conference of Catholic Bishops, for example, routinely issues policy recommendations and statements in support of legislation in Congress. However, the bishops write in *The Challenge of Peace*, "when making applications of [moral] principles we realize—and we wish readers to recognize—that prudential judgments are involved based on specific circumstances which can change or which can be interpreted differently by people of good will." Pope Paul VI, in his 1971 apostolic letter *Octogesima Adveniens* (The Eightieth Anniversary), issued a similar decree: "In the face of such widely varying situations it is difficult for us to utter a unified message and to put forward a solution which has universal validity. Such is not our ambition, nor is it our mission. It is up to the Christian communities to analyze with objectivity the situation which is proper to their own country, to shed on it the light of the Gospel's unalterable words and for action from the social teaching of the Church."

We are members of a pilgrim church, and our understanding of God's plan for our world is constantly developing in response to new historical realities. This is why we have a Catholic social tradition that responds to emerging social challenges. As lay members of our church, it is our duty to engage in this sort of dialogue as an essential component of our concern for the common good.

In this chapter, we look at a few of the most important issues of our time and offer our thoughts on how the Catholic social tradition can be brought to bear in solving them. We do not claim to speak for the leaders of the Church in presenting this agenda for the common good. Nor do we claim a sort of zealous moral certainty that holds up our agenda for the common good as the only way to achieve the Church's mission in the world. That's because we understand that there is no one public policy program that will ever fully address the social objectives of our faith. It's also because we understand that some people may rightfully disagree with us. The issues we have chosen to highlight here are by no means the only pressing moral concerns that challenge our nation and world today. We chose them in part because we feel that increased attention to and discussion of these issues are essential to advancing the common good at this particular moment in history. This agenda for the common good is the product of our own prudential judgment, using Pope John XXIII's "see, judge, act" method for applying the Catholic social tradition to the problems of our day (as we discussed in Chapter Two). It is based on three years of careful thought and consultation: conversations with political and religious leaders, as well as everyday Americans from all walks of life and all corners of the country. We propose it here as a vision of the *possible*—and not just for Catholics but for all Americans of goodwill.

Poverty: The Root of All Problems

If there's one social message to be learned from the Gospels, it's that the single greatest concern for any Christian should be helping the poor. To illustrate this point, our friend Jim Wallis sometimes uses a copy of the Bible with all the references to poverty cut out. The result is a scripture that's left in shreds. Without concern for the *other*, our faith gives us little to do in this life but sit around and think about ourselves. Poverty will always be with us, Jesus said, and so will our duty to stand in solidarity against it. We cannot escape our obligation to do everything we can to eliminate poverty's causes and lessen its effects.

While most Christians are quick to recognize our duty to help and empower the poor, what is often less apparent is the *practicality* of working to end poverty. This can be a particularly difficult concept to grasp in a country that takes pride in self-reliance and individualism, and in which we're happy to provide basic alms to those who are poor through "no fault of their own" and expect everyone else to pull themselves up by their bootstraps. If we're really serious about tackling the pressing moral concerns of our world and building a prosperous and secure future, however, we need to address the root causes of social problems—and most of the time, those root causes can be traced to poverty. Poverty is a parent of crime, disease, war, and drug abuse. It drives migration and immigration; it leads to environmental destruction; it allows terrorist leaders to recruit from the ranks of people who see few other options. A 2004 study by the Alan Guttmacher Institute found that 73 percent of U.S. women who seek an abortion do so because they feel they cannot afford a baby. There is scarcely a social ill that can't be traced to poverty, and because of this, it is absolutely impossible to address any of these problems without taking on the poverty that drives them. The sooner we accept this fact, the sooner we will be on our way to a fairer, safer, happier, and more peaceful world.

Don't get us wrong. We're not arguing that anyone who wants a free ride should be able to get one on the taxpayers' dime. It's true that any time we provide charity, there's a pretty good chance that some people are going to take advantage of our generosity. And any system for alleviating poverty must recognize that those who can work have a personal responsibility to be productive members of society. But just as providing nothing but handouts will do little to help the poor improve their situations in life, doing no more than telling people to take care of themselves will also fail to fix the problem of poverty. The poor, as Pope Benedict writes, will always need charity because charity is born of the profound sense of love and caring that no political system can ever provide. But charity, according to Saint Augustine, "is no substitute for justice withheld." Often poverty is rooted in and perpetuated by a complex array of social and economic factors: lack of education and jobs, oppressive laws and leaders, and in many cases the presence of poverty itself. Poverty begets poverty and saps communities of the ability to hope and to work for a better future. We cannot overcome poverty without addressing the injustice that causes it. Liberals and conservatives alike must take care not to be tempted to make the false choice between justice and charity. It's our responsibility to provide both.

Indeed, much of the world's poverty can be traced to *systematic* injustice, often rooted in political and economic decisions made hundreds of years ago. It's no coincidence that extremely poor countries in Africa and Latin America were colonized by European powers that took what they wanted and kept the indigenous populations in slavery. Even in today's postcolonial times, the agricultural and extractive industries in these countries are often owned by Western corporations that earn tidy profits as they pillage the land and give little back to the local populations. Their money and powerful political connections help prop up corrupt governments abroad and ensure that First World leaders enact foreign policies sympathetic to big multinational business. From diamonds to oil to sweatshop labor, oppression is still very much a reality in the twenty-first century.

For many back home, things are not all that much better. Chronic poverty in many African American communities is in large part the vestige of our own country's experience with slavery, followed by the systematic racial discrimination of "Jim Crow" laws that persisted for more than a century after the Civil War. Poverty also hurts families. Children raised in an environment of opportunity and hope have a good chance of success in life, while those born to poverty and despair have the odds stacked against them. The stress and burdens that result from parents working at multiple low-wage jobs to make ends meet or from underemployment and unemployment often undermine family life.

In the nearsighted world of the politics of division, it's easy to tolerate poverty as a necessary evil. We blame the poor for their situation, calling them too stupid or too lazy to better their lives. We use Jesus' reminder that the poor will always be with us to excuse our own lack of commitment to ending poverty. Most of all, we force ourselves to make a false choice between working to end poverty and working to secure our own prosperity. The sad reality is that very few of us actually benefit in a material sense from the disparity between rich and poor. Poverty hurts us all, and in a time when threats to the future of humanity are now manifest on a global scale—as in the case of climate change, terrorism, and nuclear destruction—we can no longer afford to ignore our less privileged brothers and sisters, no matter how far away they may be. What does the prosperous town in America have to do with the poor village in Afghanistan? As the events of September 11, 2001, taught us, the answer to this question is *everything*. The notion of the global community is no longer an ideal to be realized at a later date and time. It's the reality in which we all live today.

So what do we do about poverty? Well, for one thing, rich nations like ours can and should continue providing aid to poor countries and supporting truly integral human development. The United Nations, for instance, has set eight Millennium Development Goals (MDGs), which constitute an antipoverty blueprint supported by all 191 UN member countries as well as leading development institutions. The MDGs challenge us to eradicate extreme poverty and hunger. With one billion people on the planet living in extreme poverty, the goals call for action to achieve universal primary education; empower women and promote gender equality; reduce child mortality; improve maternal health; combat HIV/AIDS, malaria, and other diseases; ensure environmental sustainability; and develop a global partnership for development. The U.S.-based ONE Campaign (http://www.one.org) believes that by increasing our nation's foreign aid by a just a small fraction of the total U.S. budget, we can reverse global poverty. International support for fair trade, debt relief, and basic needs such as education, health, clean water, food, and care for orphans, ONE argues, is essential to addressing poverty's root causes.

As Americans, we also need to come to a better understanding of the connections between our actions at home and poverty in the world. One of the most striking examples of how U.S. policy contributes to global poverty can be found in the Farm Bill, a large piece of agricultural spending and subsidy legislation that Congress passes every five years or so. In addition to funding food stamps and school lunch programs, the bill disburses millions of dollars to large agribusiness companies, subsidizing corporations to grow a surplus of rice, corn, wheat, soybeans, and cotton. All this extra produce floods the world markets, driving down prices and wiping out local farming industries. At great expense to U.S. taxpayers, what can't be sold is packaged and shipped to poor countries as food aid.

This may sound like a nice gesture, but in reality, it does little more than trap the poor in a situation of dependence. With tons and tons of cheap food on the market, how can small farmers in developing countries ever expect to develop their own agricultural economies and lift themselves out of poverty? They can't. Faced with the prospect of starvation, many of these farmers immigrate—often illegally—to the United States, where they find low-wage jobs working on the very farms that receive the agricultural subsidies. Worse still, small farmers in the United States do not qualify for the subsidies. The only ones who benefit are large farming operations, some of whom perpetuate the system by kicking back millions to lawmakers through their lobbies. In 2007, President Bush offered an approach to help level the playing field by limiting Farm Bill subsidies to landowners reporting less than $200,000 of adjusted gross income (AGI) on their tax returns. But the Democratic-controlled Congress bowed to pressure from the agribusiness lobbies and changed the limit to $750,000 in the Senate version and $1 million in the House version.

Addressing poverty on our own soil will also require us to look seriously at its root causes and to solutions that incorporate both charity and justice. Catholic Charities USA (CCUSA) has launched a campaign to reduce poverty in America by 50 percent by the year 2020. The campaign's 2007 founding document, *Poverty: Threat to the Common Good*, notes that among the industrialized nations, the United States has one of the highest poverty rates (thirty-seven million Americans—and one of every six children—are poor) and one of the lowest spending rates on poverty reduction. CCUSA identifies two key weaknesses in our current policies: lack of living-wage jobs and lack of adequate social welfare policies.

The campaign calls on the federal government to implement policy changes to address these weaknesses, including efforts to create more living-wage jobs, to raise existing wages (including the minimum wage), and to invest in social policies that support low-income families and individuals. These policy investments should, among other things, strengthen our nutrition safety net, extend the Temporary Assistance for Needy Families (TANF) program to benefit more families, ensure universal health insurance coverage, increase access to education and training, and create more affordable housing. To assist in paying for these policy changes, CCUSA "supports progressive tax policies that will benefit lower and middle income taxpayers while asking those who have more to pay more." In the spirit of the Catholic social tradition, they reject the proposition that "agencies such as ours" should substitute for some of the basic functions of government—a notion that runs contrary to the principles of President Bush's "compassionate conservatism" social welfare plan.

One of the clearest ways that injustice leads to poverty is manifest in our educational system. It's impossible to break the cycle of poverty when schools in poor areas are chronically underfunded and those in wealthy parts are able to pay top dollar for facilities and talent. Anyone who works intimately with people struggling to escape poverty will tell you that a first step is access to a good education. We can't ensure this education unless we're prepared to make a serious commitment to fix our nation's failing school systems, through both financial and structural changes. Sadly, our leaders have offered the exact opposite in recent years: the ironically named No Child Left Behind Act that actually penalizes poorly performing schools.

We need to provide real incentives for work. Despite the fact that unskilled workers often work the hardest, in our society's most physically demanding and most undesirable jobs, many struggle to feed their kids. Even toiling for sixty hours a week, a worker will scarcely make more than $20,000 a year at the July 2008 minimum wage of $6.55 per hour—still below the federal poverty level for a family of four. If the market can't provide a living wage, then it's up to our lawmakers to enact legislation that compels the market to pay workers what they deserve. The USCCB has consistently called for a living wage as an essential component of a social policy that respects the life and dignity of all persons.

Our nation also needs to respect the rights of workers to organize unions to improve wages or ensure respect in the workplace. Not only is the right to collective bargaining essential to creating a fair and equitable free market, it's something repeatedly affirmed by the Catholic Church. "No one may deny the right to organize without attacking human dignity itself," wrote the U.S. Catholic Bishops in their 1986 pastoral letter *Economic Justice for All*. "Therefore, we firmly oppose organized efforts, such as those regrettably seen in this country, to break existing unions or prevent workers from organizing." When Chris worked as a union organizer after college, he saw firsthand the lengths to which some unscrupulous employers are prepared to go to deny this right, firing and intimidating workers who try to form a union. Unfortunately, our current laws give only a slap on the wrist to those employers who break them. In 2007, a bill called the Employee Free Choice Act was introduced in Congress to improve worker protections and make it easier for workers who want a union to be able to have one.

Abortion

As the USCCB reminds us in its 2008 *Faithful Citizenship* document, abortion is one of the preeminent threats to human life in our society today. Each abortion constitutes a direct attack on human life, and so we have a special moral obligation to work to end or reduce the practice of abortion to the greatest extent possible. But as we have noted in earlier chapters, something is seriously wrong with the abortion dialogue in America today. While most Americans want to address the issue in civil and constructive ways that respect the life, dignity, and freedom of all involved, vocal culture warriors at both ends of the political spectrum continue to insist on a contentious and unproductive debate. It's time for both sides of this debate to stop screaming at each other and work together to forge solutions that people of goodwill can get behind. Only through this kind of dialogue and compromise can we as Catholics realize our goal of building a society that truly values and protects human life at all levels and at all stages.

Too often in our nation's discourse on human life, the public is presented with a very limited and false choice: either we can fight to end abortion, or we can fight to promote social justice. But most Americans see the need for a different approach. They have grave concerns about the morality of abortion, but they also realize that many women (especially single women) feel trapped by the burdens of modern society. These Americans see that abortion and social justice do not represent an either-or proposition; rather, the two are intricately related: the solution to abortion *is* social justice.

Pope John Paul II in *Evangelium Vitae* (The Gospel of Life) recognized this essential connection when he called for the elimination of the underlying causes of threats to human life "especially by ensuring proper support for families and motherhood." He also insisted it was necessary to rethink "labour, urban, residential and social service policies so as to harmonize working schedules with time available for the family, so that it becomes effectively possible to take care of children and the elderly."

The USCCB reminds us in the 2007 revision of the *Faithful Citizenship* document that when—as in the current political and cultural climate—abortion can't be made illegal, we can and should turn our focus to practical solutions:

> Sometimes morally flawed laws already exist. In this situation, the process of framing legislation to protect life is subject to prudential judgment and "the art of the possible." At times this process may restore justice only partially or gradually. For example, Pope John Paul II taught that when a government official who fully opposes abortion cannot succeed in completely overturning a pro-abortion law, he or she may work to improve protection for unborn human life, "limiting the harm done by such a law" and lessening its negative impact as much as possible.

Along similar lines, Father Richard John Neuhaus affirmed the acceptability of prudence in arriving at solutions to fully promote and protect human life. As he stated on NBC's *Meet the Press* in 2006, "If you have a senator ... or a congressperson who says, 'Yes, I agree that the goal is and, as a Catholic, I am convinced in conscience that the goal is every unborn child protected in law and welcomed in life, but I disagree with the bishops as to how we might get to that goal,' that is a different thing and ... his or her relationship with the church is not compromised or impaired."

The connection between poverty and abortion is not theoretical. History shows that one of the most effective ways to deal with abortion is to address its underlying economic (and cultural) factors. According to 2008 Alan Guttmacher Institute statistics, U.S. abortion rates declined significantly during the prosperous 1990s and continued that trend from 2000 to 2005, though at a slower pace of decline. This progress strongly suggests that economic and social factors contribute to reducing abortion rates. Indeed, a Catholics United study based on Kansas data showed that counties with lower unemployment, greater health insurance coverage, and more Head Start centers have measurably lower abortion rates (you can find the report at http://www.catholics-united.org/abortion-study). Globally, some of the lowest abortion rates are found in countries like the Netherlands and Germany—in which abortion is generally legal but health care and economic assistance are available to all women and families, and in which economic pressures are not nearly as strong as they are in the United States. Poor countries tend to have higher abortion rates, even in those where abortion is illegal. In poverty-stricken Brazil, for instance, abortion is strictly prohibited, yet an astounding forty of every thousand pregnancies end in abortion. The current rate of U.S. abortions is about half that of Brazil.

Culture warriors in America will argue that to be pro-life, we must ensure that the unborn are protected under the law. This would indeed be an ideal situation. But legal status doesn't always realize the goal that we desire. For example, by the culture warriors' logic, Brazil, with its high (illegal) abortion rate, is more pro-life than the Netherlands, with its low (legal) rate. Clearly, however, the facts tell a different story. Where the unborn are concerned, it is absolutely crucial for us to focus on policies that will work *right now* as well as in the future, and that will truly realize the goal we desire: a society that supports, protects, and values human life at all stages.

In recent years, many members of Congress have dedicated their energies to passing legislation aimed specifically at combating the root causes of abortion. They are not all perfect; some include contraception—which the Church opposes. In 2007, Senator Robert Casey Jr. (D-Pa.) and Representative Lincoln Davis (D-Tenn.) introduced the Pregnant Women's Support Act in the U.S. Senate and House of Representatives, respectively. The measure, which does not include contraception funding, aims to reduce the number of abortions by 95 percent in ten years through a host of economic and social measures, including outlawing the designation of pregnancy as a noncovered preexisting condition in health insurance plans. Earlier that year, Representatives Tim Ryan (D-Ohio) and Rosa De Lauro (D-Conn.)

worked to pass a $647 million economic aid package in the House intended to prevent unintended pregnancies and support pregnant women. By providing health care, child care, adoption, and job support to women and families, it reduces the economic burdens of child rearing and helps women continue their education when faced with an unexpected pregnancy.

The Global Climate Crisis

Our faith has always emphasized the Christian responsibility to care for all of creation, and our church leaders have increasingly urged constructive action to address the environmental and climate crises as an urgent demand of the global common good. Finally, the world is awakening to the reality of the climate crisis. This issue is of particular concern to Catholics. That's because it is absolutely impossible to build a culture of life if we don't have a healthy planet. The potential effects of climate change include food and water shortages, violent weather, and disease. Melting glaciers are already raising the sea level around the world, and a rise of just a few feet could trigger a humanitarian crisis of epic proportions as hundreds of millions of people flee coastal flooding. "Poor nations and sectors of society are particularly vulnerable to the adverse consequences of climate change, due to lesser resources and capacity to mitigate their effects and adapt to altered surroundings," Pope Benedict XVI told the United Nations in 2007. Global climate change now poses a direct threat to human life, a threat that will only worsen if we do not take steps to address it.

Although the evidence points overwhelmingly to human causes of climate change—primarily the release of carbon dioxide into the atmosphere through the burning of fossil fuels—our nation's leaders have made little progress toward addressing the root causes of the problem. What we need are smaller cars that get better gas mileage and use new energy-saving technologies. We need more public transportation and more conservation.

We need to make investments in new sources of electrical power—like solar and wind—and stop kowtowing to big energy lobbies who dazzle us with oxymoronic ideas like "clean coal," forcing us into the false choice between using fossil fuels and a having strong economy.

It's true that consumers must start to make greener choices and be willing to pay for them too. But it's also true that our elected leaders need to start crafting policies that seek what's best for future generations. It can be done. In the 1980s, when polar ozone holes were traced to the release of chlorofluorocarbons (CFCs) from aerosol propellants, governments around the world banded together and agreed to take measures to limit production of the harmful chemicals. In Brazil, public policy measures have created a burgeoning ethanol economy to replace fossil fuels in automobiles. Today, ethanol accounts for 30 percent of Brazil's fuel consumption.

Cutting carbon emissions is good not only for the environment but also for the economy. The U.S. Department of Energy estimates that more than three hundred thousand new jobs would be created if the United States generated 20 percent of its electricity needs from renewable sources such as wind and solar power. Brazil's ethanol program itself created hundreds of thousands of new jobs and helped keep money that consumers spend on energy within the national economy rather than going overseas. Converting to a renewable energy economy would not only help U.S. workers but would also reduce our near-absolute dependence on foreign oil, thereby eliminating the source of many global conflicts, particularly in the Middle East. And last but not least, investment in public transportation would reduce traffic and help rejuvenate local communities. Studies have shown that transit-oriented development—structuring communities around public transportation systems—provides considerable economic benefits, and workers who commute using public transportation save money and experience less stress than those who drive. Our public policy can be used to foster public transportation growth and smarter development. In some U.S. cities, for example, home buyers can qualify for better mortgage terms if they buy in proximity to public transportation.

Despite overwhelming evidence that human beings are causing climate change, that the United States is the single biggest contributor, and that a majority of Americans want our nation to take action, policymakers have been slow to address climate change as a major issue. Some refuse to act until they have "indisputable proof" that there is a problem. By then, it will be too late.

Health Care

The Catholic social tradition teaches that health care is a fundamental human right, and so we have an essential responsibility to ensure that all have access to safe, quality, affordable health care. Health care is essential to the common good because we all fare better when everyone has access to it, thereby improving the health of our society in general. As the only industrialized nation in the world that does not guarantee its citizens health care, the United States clearly has some catching up to do.

Opponents of universal health care often claim that it equates to "socialized medicine," a system in which the government manages and pays for all aspects of health care. But this is not necessarily the case. In 2006, for example, Massachusetts passed a law requiring its citizens to carry health care coverage, offering a reduced-rate plan for low- and middle-income residents to make this requirement easier to fulfill. Employers who do not provide coverage to their workers are required to pay an annual premium to help defray the cost of the subsidized plans. Massachusetts's universal health care plan—which preserves the outstanding medical care of the state's private health system—is just one possible solution to this growing crisis. The point is that there are ways to maintain our existing health care infrastructure while ensuring that all Americans have access to the care they need.

In any universal health care system, a certain amount of public funds will likely be used to cover the uninsured, and some people may ask why taxpayers with health care should be required to pick up the tab for those who go without. This is a fair question, and the answer again is the common good: we *all* benefit when our fellow citizens are covered, and we *all* suffer when they aren't. It really is that simple. For some forty-seven million uninsured Americans, the emergency room has become the high-priced replacement for the doctor's office. And since hospitals in most of the country cannot turn away emergency patients even if these patients can't pay, many hospitals wind up writing off expensive emergency costs. Who pays in the end? We all do, in the form of higher insurance premiums and poorer service. Lack of preventive care and regular checkups only worsen the problem, because by the time many uninsured people finally see a doctor, their treatment costs more than it would have had the problem been caught earlier. Lost days at work also hurt our businesses, preventable disabilities place burdens on our troubled Social Security and Medicare systems, and worrying about health security hurts our families. U.S. businesses also lose their edge in the global marketplace when they have to compete against companies whose governments do help shoulder their workers' health care costs. And as we noted earlier, lack of heath care coverage is a major contributing factor to abortions in the United States.

There are important reasons for using public funds to promote certain aspects of the common good, and health care is one of them. Through our government, we guarantee all Americans a secondary education, we provide a system of roads to get around on, and when our freedom is in jeopardy, we provide for our national defense. Do we then say that we have socialized education, socialized highways, and socialized defense? Of course not. It's time for us to modernize our thinking on health policy and ensure that all Americans have access to the care they need. The only thing standing in the way of this is our leaders' lack of political will.

War

When the United States invaded Iraq in 2003, it did so against the conviction and advice of many of our nation's religious communities, including the president's own United Methodist Church and, of course, the Catholic Church. On the eve of the war, Pope John Paul II called for a renewed focus on diplomatic solutions and urged world leaders to go to war only as a last resort. This followed a late 2002 statement from the USCCB expressing serious concerns that the impending invasion did not meet the criteria of the Catholic "just war" tradition. "We are concerned," the bishops wrote, "that war against Iraq could have unpredictable consequences not only for Iraq but for peace and stability elsewhere in the Middle East. The use of force might provoke the very kinds of attacks that it is intended to prevent, could impose terrible new burdens on an already long-suffering civilian population, and could lead to wider conflict and instability in the region."

It took several years for the Republican and Democratic leaders who rushed us to war to admit that they had made a serious mistake, and by then, it was too late to undo all the damage that had been done. The war failed to achieve our nation's stated objectives in a reasonable time period; it resulted in the deaths of thousands of U.S. troops and hundreds of thousands of Iraqi civilians; it created a terrible humanitarian crisis; and it contributed to further instability in an already volatile region. Back home, the war placed a severe strain on the U.S. economy and diminished our country's ability to tend to crises on our own soil. Equipment that could have been used to aid in the Hurricane Katrina recovery was either tied up on the front lines or broken down at home. When massive wildfires hit southern California in the fall of 2007, aid efforts were similarly hindered.

And then there's our national security. The war in Iraq was supposedly fought to help rid the world of terror; in reality, it only made things worse. On the eve of the war, the notorious al-Qaeda terrorist network was holed up in the hills of Afghanistan with no connection whatsoever to Iraq, but the instability we created soon provided perfect conditions for the group to become entrenched in the streets of Baghdad. Through its actions in Iraq, the United States only reinforced its reputation as the world's schoolyard bully. Whatever goodwill existed toward us in the wake of the awful events of 9/11 was squandered in a war that we didn't need to fight.

If there's anything positive to be gained from the Iraq experience, it's the knowledge that we must never again rush to war under such dubious circumstances. "War is not always inevitable," Pope John Paul II stated in 2003, but "it is always a defeat for humanity." "Just" war does have a place in the Catholic tradition, but it may be used only as a last resort and must be fought under the right conditions. According to the teachings of the Church, a just war does not mean that we're right in using force as long as our intent is to achieve good results. On the contrary, just war teaching holds that war is acceptable only if it meets a set of very specific criteria. According to the *Catechism of the Catholic Church*, in order to go to war:

> The damage inflicted by the aggressor on the nation or community of nations must be lasting, grave, and certain;
> All other means of putting an end to it must have been shown to be impractical or ineffective;
> There must be serious prospects of success;
> The use of arms must not produce evils and disorders graver than the evil to be eliminated. The power of modern means of destruction weighs very heavily in evaluating this condition.

Just war doctrine also states that war must be waged by a "legitimate authority" (in the case of the Iraq War, the USCCB insisted that this was the United Nations), and that war must be conducted in a way that minimizes civilian casualties. As the bishops wrote in 2002, "In assessing whether 'collateral damage' is proportionate, the lives of Iraqi men, women and children should be valued as we would the lives of members of our own family and citizens of our own country." In a 2003 interview, Cardinal Joseph Ratzinger (now Pope Benedict XVI) had stronger words. "There were not sufficient reasons to unleash a war against Iraq," he said. "To say nothing of the fact that, given the new weapons that make possible destructions that go beyond the combatant groups, today we should be asking ourselves if it is still licit to admit the very existence of a 'just war.' "

America wound up in Iraq not because diplomacy failed us but because we failed diplomacy. We also wound up there because we turned our backs on the international community and pursued a "go-it-alone" strategy designed only to serve our own interests. As faithful Americans, we must never allow this to happen again. America's status as the world's only remaining superpower does not give it moral license to do whatever it pleases. On the contrary, it brings greater responsibility. "From everyone to whom much has been given," we read in Luke 12:48, "much will be required; and from one to whom much has been entrusted, even more will be demanded." This is true both in our personal lives and in how our nation behaves on the world stage.

Immigration

A shameful new front in the culture war is the recent rise of an organized effort to blame undocumented immigrants for many of the social problems our nation faces. Don't get us wrong, illegal immigration *is* a serious problem—for both the immigrants themselves and the communities whose infrastructures are taxed by throngs of new arrivals. But the response of many conservative leaders to this problem has not aligned with a Christian worldview. Instead of treating immigrants with compassion and understanding and working to correct the vast disparities of wealth and poverty globally that drive them to migrate, the culture warriors have instead chosen to demonize immigrants, claiming that the problem is best addressed by border fences and harsher penalties for those who break the law.

How easy it is to forget that most native-born Americans are themselves descended from immigrants and that the arrival of Europeans on American shores was part of a gigantic wave of unwelcome immigration! As long as the United States remains the most prosperous nation in human history, other peoples will want to claim their right to participate in that prosperity. We have a simple choice: either share that wealth abroad or share that wealth at home. There are no other options.

Anyone who has lived or traveled in Central America has experienced firsthand the crushing poverty that drives immigration. For most migrants, remaining in the native land means at best a life of suffering and at worst a premature death. America offers jobs and opportunity—a glowing chance for the immigrant to make a better life. How else can we explain the risks immigrants are willing to take with their own lives: stuffing themselves into container ships and airplane wheel wells or braving hundreds of miles of unforgiving desert? It doesn't matter how high we build the wall. As long as people are living in extreme poverty, they will seek a way to find opportunity in the United States.

The Catholic Church teaches that any immigration policy must respect first and foremost the life and dignity of the human person. Nations like ours have the right to protect our borders, the Church believes, but we also have an obligation to keep families together and to address the material poverty that forces immigrants to seek a better life. We have already seen how policies like the U.S. Farm Bill are contributing directly to this migration. We must also begin to rethink the wisdom of so-called free trade legislation, which is often designed to improve the bottom lines of multinational businesses and contains little explicit concern for those who need the most help.

By papering over the true causes of immigration and by using the issue to divide voters rather than addressing the actual causes of the problem, culture warriors are only making the things worse. If we're serious about fixing our immigration system, we need to get serious about what's wrong to begin with.

In the *Faithful Citizenship* documents, the USCCB has identified scores of issues with profound bearing on the common good. From racism to embryonic stem cell research, from euthanasia to war, abortion, and poverty, our faith calls us to address all of these important contemporary concerns with an eye toward human dignity and the common good. In formulating policy that addresses these issues, we have to keep in mind our duty to provide prudent and workable polices that will achieve real results in the real world. It is important to take stands against injustice and to work with others to create and support solutions that will help realize the vision of the Catholic social tradition.

6

Practicing the Common Good

Building a nation for all requires us to work to advance the common good at all levels of our society. It requires *public policies* that put the needs of everyone above the interests of a select few. It requires a *culture* that places concern for one another ahead of materialism, greed, and excessive individualism. It requires an *economy* measured fundamentally by the status of the poor, not just the size of the stock market or the soaring profits of large corporations. And it requires that we, as *individuals*, live our lives in ways that reflect a profound concern for one another.

These four aspects of our society—government, culture, the economy, and individuals—are fundamentally interrelated. The values we emphasize in our culture and individual lives are reflected in our government and our economic policies. Likewise, when these values are ingrained in our tax system and government, they affect individuals, families, and the vibrancy of our culture. It is for this reason that we must be prepared to address each of these components in order to build a society for the common good. Public policy that rewards personal profit at the expense of others, for example, breeds an economic system that works against the common good. It creates a culture in which wealth, power, and acquisition are the sole measures of a successful and productive life. To meet these expectations, we find ourselves "looking out for number one" in our personal lives, making material success our top priority. Because we have bought into the go-it-alone culture, we will base our votes for political leaders on what they can do for *us* rather than what they can inspire us to do for *everyone*. This further erodes public policies that would otherwise protect and advance the common good.

By contrast, if we truly believe that our nation works best when we all work together, the pieces of a society for the common good can start to fall into place. Public policy will ensure that all Americans have access to health care, a living wage, and a decent education—including a top-notch college education that everyone can afford. We'll stop settling for an economy that leaves millions behind as it heralds the growing gap between rich and poor as evidence of a healthy "free" market. And our culture will stop defining success by the size of our houses and cars and start defining it by our character and contributions as human beings. Liberated from the pressing need to always "get ahead," we'll have more time for our families, friends, and communities.

The Catholic vision of the common good calls for a kind of social change that cannot happen overnight; it requires serious reexamination of the ways we live our lives and relate to one another. The common good isn't just a collection of policies and ideas. It's a *practice* in which we must all participate. It involves our voting decisions, our economic choices, the cars we buy, the resources we use, how we treat our friends and strangers—indeed, even the ways we care for our own physical and mental well-being. It requires leaders who have the courage of conviction to stand up for what is right and challenge us to aspire to a higher moral standard. It necessitates that we all participate in our communities and government, remain vigilant against excessive materialism and greed, and be prepared to sacrifice our time and even money when the common good requires it. "Ask not what your country can do for you," John F. Kennedy said, "ask what you can do for your country." These words are as true in our time as they were in his.

Skeptics like to say that human beings are essentially incapable of putting the needs of others above their own desires. This pessimistic view of human nature is often presented as justification for an unregulated free market (which we've never really had, anyway) and for the pervasive belief that society just works best when we look out for ourselves. In fact, there are plenty of places in the world—indeed, in our own country—that operate by a core belief in concern for the common good. In many of our cities and towns, churches remain centers of strong community life, and successful new and old immigrant communities have thrived in America because their members understand the need to look out for one another. On an international scale, most industrialized countries provide health care and college education for their citizens, as well as job training for the unemployed and work schedules that allow families to spend time together. As we discussed in earlier chapters, our own country once held much more tightly to the common good, as reflected, for example, in President Franklin D. Roosevelt's New Deal reforms of the 1930s.

Even if concern for the common good is not a value that all human beings are born with, it is a value we all must learn if we are to build and maintain a healthy and productive society. Unfortunately, in the age of the politics of division exactly the opposite seems true. Corporate interests constantly bombard us with calls to consume more and more while at the same time our elected officials provide legal loopholes for these same corporations to pocket record profits while underpaying workers at home—or seeking cheaper labor abroad and taking American jobs away altogether.

The current debate over health care is a perfect example of how we must teach and learn common good values. Many Americans are suspicious of so-called universal health care, having been subjected to years of propaganda from drug and insurance companies who benefit from our expensive and outdated system. We've been led to believe that health care for everyone will mean higher costs, poorer service, and fewer choices for consumers. These attitudes stand in stark contrast to the views of many British or Canadian citizens who, brought up in societies that provide quality health care free of charge to everyone, cannot imagine living their lives without such benefits. In fact, Americans pay the most but get the least health care bang for their buck.

Have these countries suffered because of their belief in the common good? Not at all. As the U.S. economy faltered through 2007—dragged down by five years of war, deficit spending, and a banking crisis fueled by real estate speculators and questionable mortgage-lending practices—other Western nations were booming. Europe's currency reached all-time highs against the U.S. dollar and threatened to replace the greenback as the standard for the rest of the world. Canadians began streaming to the United States to exercise their own newfound spending power. And London cemented its role as a major global financial center, prompting the *Independent* newspaper to declare it the new "capital of the world." Prosperity and the common good are not conflicting ideas. On the contrary, one cannot exist without the other.

As we have noted, one of the hallmarks of the politics of division is that it presents us with a collection of false choices—national security *or* civil liberties, good health care *or* health care for everyone, a strong economy *or* a thriving natural environment. By forcing us to view these choices as either-or propositions, the politics of division mistakenly convinces us that we cannot hope to build a society for the common good without giving up on our individual success. These false choices obscure a set of *real* choices that confront our society every day and challenge us to adopt the practices of the common good instead of the practices of the politics of division. We must choose whether we should act with conviction or cowardice, engage in civility or destruction, opt for compromise or obstruction, and use persuasion or coercion. The first set of choices—conviction, civility, compromise, and persuasion—are practices vital to building a society for the common good. The other choices—cowardice, destruction, obstruction, and coercion—are essential components of the politics of division. They thrive in a go-it-alone culture, and they have been getting us nowhere fast.

Conviction or Cowardice?

Politics used to be about a great debate of ideas. But in a fast-paced media world, it often seems that our leaders care more about getting elected than they care about building the common good. Instead of telling us what they believe, it seems, they're just telling us what we want to hear—or what they *think* we want to hear. Indeed, the prevalence of polling and focus groups in formulating political messages leaves many of us feeling like political consumers rather than participants in the great experiment of democracy. Candidates market themselves just like companies market products. They even use the same techniques: TV commercials, Internet ads, the media, market research. It's all about getting our vote so that they can stay in office.

Why don't enough of our leaders speak from their heart about who they are and what they believe? Simply put, it's because they are afraid—afraid of losing elections and losing control. This is not to say that our leaders are just a bunch of power-hungry political careerists who seek elected offices for their own personal gain (although, to be sure, there are some who fit that bill!). But it is to say that in their apprehension, these leaders have accepted a false choice between acting with conviction and getting elected when their real choice should be between acting with conviction and acting with fear.

Those who adopt watered-down political platforms that seek to appease everyone run the risk of doing little good for anyone—particularly for whatever of their own true beliefs got swept to the side in the rush to construct "safe" campaign messages. Ironically, this practice tends to alienate the very voters it purports to attract. In the 2004 presidential election, George W. Bush managed to portray himself as a strong and decisive leader who took firm stands even on unpopular issues. John Kerry was cast as a "flip-flopper" whose positions were in constant flux. Although this was almost certainly an unfair characterization, the apparent disparity between Kerry's personal beliefs and his campaign promises was bewildering to many voters. "I cannot tell you how deeply I respect the belief about life and when it begins," he responded when asked about public funding for abortion during the second presidential debate. "But I can't take what is an article of faith for me and legislate it for someone who doesn't share that article of faith." Many Catholics, including Catholic Democrats, were perplexed by Senator Kerry's inability to answer this question in a way that demonstrated how he would put his personal value for life into action in some way. Bush, on the other hand, responded with conviction: "My answer is, we're not going to spend taxpayers' money on abortion." He then called on the nation to find common ground. "This is an issue that divides America," he said. "But certainly reasonable people can agree on how to reduce abortions in America."

A fear of speaking with conviction and moral clarity is alienating to many who would otherwise support the agenda for the common good because they are left feeling that our leaders don't know what they believe and therefore that they lack conviction. Democrat Robert Casey Jr. of Pennsylvania realized this when running for U.S. Senate in 2006 in a state deeply divided between pro-life and pro-choice constituencies. Casey took the issue head on: "You can't have it both ways and say, 'I am pro-choice but . . . ,' or 'I am pro-life but . . . ,'" he said of his own position on abortion. In this way, Casey cut through the politics of division and found a way to appeal to both pro-life and pro-choice voters. He accomplished this not by speaking from both sides of his mouth but by finding common ground and focusing on the issue's root causes (lack of health care and economic support for women and families) instead of the lightning rod of whether or not abortion should be illegal. Voters responded, choosing Democrat Casey over Catholic Republican Rick Santorum in part because Casey's beliefs—his convictions—were clear and meshed with his political views.

We're blessed with other public officials who embrace conviction over fear. Even though Republican Senator Chuck Hagel of Nebraska voted to allow President Bush to go to war in Iraq, he called consistently for an end to the war when it became apparent that force was not achieving our national objectives in the region—despite the fact that this stand could have hurt him in the polls and within his party. Democrat Tim Kaine won the 2005 Virginia governor's race as an anti–death penalty candidate, even though most Virginia voters favored capital punishment. When the opposition ran attack ads claiming that he believed "Adolf Hitler doesn't qualify for the death penalty," Kaine stuck to his guns, citing his own Catholic conviction that all human life is sacred. Republican senator Olympia Snowe of Maine has taken unpopular stands within her party on several occasions, opposing the size of President Bush's 2003 tax cuts, for example, and challenging the administration's handling of the war in Iraq. In 2005, she participated in the famous bipartisan "Gang of 14" compromise, which ended a contentious impasse over Supreme Court nominations.

We also face choices between conviction and cowardice in our economy, our culture, and our own personal lives. When we buy into the go-it-alone culture of excessive materialism and greed, do we do so because we believe that having bigger houses, higher salaries, and longer commutes will make us better or happier people, or because we're afraid that in avoiding the rat race, we will be missing out? As individuals, we all need to take a continuous and serious look at the ways in which we live our lives and have the courage to give up the things that are detracting from our health and our families.

Civility or Destruction?

Anyone who has competed on a college or high school debate team learned the rules of civil debate and argument. Unlike today's politics and our shouting-match talk shows, the victors in competitive debates were determined on the merits of their arguments, the soundness of their positions, and their rhetorical skills. Whatever happened to civil and substantive argument, the kind that used to prevail even between deeply opposed political rivals? Or to the belief that engaging in civil debate regarding bold and passionately felt differences could be constructive and fruitful, leading to innovative solutions that neither side could have reached on its own?

In recent years, the practice of civil debate—a cornerstone of our democracy and a requirement of the common good—has been replaced by the practice of personal and political destruction. These vicious and disparaging tactics distract us from the substantive differences among opposing points of view and the different philosophical assumptions or policy positions they reflect. The politics of destruction opts to attack the messenger of a contrary opinion instead of intelligently and politely—civilly—challenging the merits of the policy position or argument. Destruction seeks not to disassemble the debater's ideas but rather to annihilate his or her character, credibility, or personality.

The Bush administration mounted a classic campaign of destruction when it was collecting data to justify going to war in Iraq. As part of related intelligence gathering, the Central Intelligence Agency sent a former U.S. ambassador, Joseph Wilson, to Niger to investigate reports that Iraq had sought to buy uranium there for use in weapons of mass destruction. Wilson found no evidence to support this claim, but President Bush still chose to use it to bolster his case for going to war. When Wilson later challenged the administration in a 2003 New York Times opinion piece, the destruction campaign began. Rather than disputing Wilson's argument or the evidence, the White House attacked Wilson's credibility. As part of that process, it used the media to reveal that Wilson's wife, Valerie Plame, was a CIA operative. Because Plame may have been involved in facilitating her husband's mission, the White House suggested, Wilson's findings were invalid. In effect, the administration destroyed a messenger who advanced an honest but unfavorable argument, showing little regard for the implications on national security, the safety of Plame's sources, and the integrity of the CIA. In a well-publicized legal case, a White House official named Lewis "Scooter" Libby took the fall for the administration's leak of Plame's identity—but the politics of destruction claimed victory over civil argument and hard evidence. As it turns out, campaigns of personal and political destruction often don't serve our national interest or the common good. By obscuring rational debate and argument, the destruction approach helped send us into and keep us engaged in a costly war based on weak evidence of the existence of weapons of mass destruction that indeed were nowhere to be found in Iraq.

Civility is essential to the kinds of constructive debate and honest deliberations that fortify any functional democracy. Democracy is built on the understanding that there are indeed differences among people, values, and political approaches. But it also holds that through civil deliberation and rational argument, we can discuss these differences and forge new solutions based on respect for all views and engagement with all parties. Civility and respect are key to our marriages and personal relationships as well: we all know from personal experience that when disrespect, scorn, or abuse toward another person become the norm in a family or a marriage, it's hard to find peace or any practical solutions at all.

Civility is in fact a very Christian practice. It flows from the essential belief that we are all created in God's image and are therefore worthy of respect and decent treatment from our fellow human beings. Even though we may disagree, even passionately, on numerous matters, we don't seek to demolish other people's character or integrity. We challenge their opinions or their arguments, not their very being. Civility should not be seen as a muzzle that would stifle us from expressing and fighting for our deeply held convictions. Nor is it a harness that should restrict us from fighting back when our position or character is challenged or even attacked by others. But when we do fight back, we should always seek the high ground and answer these challenges and personal attacks in a spirit of civility and conviction, and not a spirit of fear or personal destruction.

Older members of Congress often reminisce about the days when legislators from both sides of the aisle met for drinks or social dinners after work. These moments helped politicians of vastly different stripes cultivate bonds of friendship and mutual respect that set the tone for more constructive debate and negotiations during long days of legislating. Sometimes creative give-and-take solutions or breakthrough compromises were forged over late-night dinners or card games where civility and trust developed despite political and ideological differences. As we noted in Chapter Three, Republican President Ronald Reagan and Democratic Speaker of the House Tip O'Neill, in a spirit of civility and rational debate, hammered out a compromise that improved Social Security. Today, Justices Ruth Bader Ginsburg and Antonin Scalia, ideological opposites on the Supreme Court, cultivate a friendship outside the Court—attending opera performances together and sharing a strong commitment to their families. This kind of civility, more prevalent in the not-too-distant past than it is in the present day, helped our government get things done despite strong differences of opinion or approach. In our families and marriages, we also know that shared experiences and time together foster trust and civility, which are essential to resolving differences.

In 2007, a group of prominent lay Catholic citizens from both sides of the political aisle came together to issue a statement of guidelines affirming their commitment to the practice of civility in the public square. More than seventy former ambassadors, senators, members of Congress, past chairs of both the Republican and Democratic parties, and other prominent Catholic citizens have signed "A Catholic Call to Observe Civility in Political Debate." The project was coordinated by two Catholic University of America classmates and friends: Ambassador Thomas Melady, a lifelong Republican and former ambassador to the Vatican, and Washington attorney Timothy May, a lifelong Democrat and lead campaign staffer for John F. Kennedy. Their mutual respect and friendship provided the spirit behind this Catholic Civility Project. Several Catholics in Alliance board members and leaders also signed on.

The guidelines of the Civility Project recognized the deep divisions and differences that exist among Catholic citizens, and emphasized the need for Catholics to debate their differences in public life with courtesy and respect. The signers discouraged Catholics from enlisting the "Church's moral endorsement for our political preferences." They also discouraged Catholic citizens from using Communion for partisan political gain. "*Civility for Catholics*," the statement concluded, "as for all believers, is grounded in the teachings of the Lord, who demands [that] we love one another as we love ourselves, that we be kind, and that we forgive. From this teaching flows the command to respect even a bitter opponent … and to not use the Church for one's political purposes." You can find out more about the Catholic Civility Project and register your support at http://www.catholiccivility.org.

Compromise or Disengagement?

In Chapter Three, we showed that representing the values of our faith in the public discourse is possible only when we are willing to make compromises. This principle works for all aspects of our society, not just for politics. Compromise is a value many of us learn as children on the playground: we have to give and take a little bit, or else our favorite toy ends up in shreds and no one is happy. And anyone who's been married for any length of time will attest that without compromise, relationships cannot flourish. Is it possible to create a political system in which compromise does not exist? Indeed it is: Adolf Hitler did it in Germany, Fidel Castro in Cuba, and Saddam Hussein in Iraq. Democracy without compromise is not democracy at all.

The common good suffers when we refuse even to participate in dialogue, to civilly discuss our differences at all—when a "my way or the highway" approach leads us to disengage. We have seen the practice of disengagement ruin our political process and erode the common good, and we've seen it ruin marriages and communities. When one spouse just starts doing whatever he or she wants without concern for the other, the marriage and the family suffer. In politics, when deeply divided adversaries disengage from dialogue with each other, progress on important concerns can grind to a halt. Disengagement does not advance the common good. Far from being a solution, it only makes our problems worse.

The abortion debate serves as an excellent example of what happens when disengagement triumphs over compromise. This conversation has become so polarized that real commonsense social, economic, and cultural efforts that would actually prevent and reduce abortions—widely supported by most Americans—have been pushed to the margins in favor of continuing the polarizing and paralyzing debate (a pretty good fundraising tactic for all involved). For decades, these two sides have hurled angry rhetoric at each other from opposite corners of the room, coming to the table to hammer out agreements only on rare occasions, if at all.

As we discussed in Chapter Five, through dialogue and com- promise our lawmakers introduced several breakthrough bills in 2007 aimed at reducing and preventing abortions. These bills provided the kinds of social, cultural, and economic supports for women and families that have proved to reduce abortions both in this country and elsewhere. Neither bill required either side in the abortion debate to relinquish its values. Both seek to address and eliminate the root causes of abortion and create essential conditions for a culture of life, something the American people desperately want and something our faith and the common good require.

Disengagement from diverse points of view and uncompromising approaches can have disastrous consequences. Before President George W. Bush went to war in Iraq in March 2003, he had disengaged for more than a year from everyone, at home and abroad, who opposed his plans to go to war. Aid agencies, Middle East experts, diplomats, activists, our church, and many others challenged the wisdom of a "preventive" and immediate war of "first resort" and urged pursuit of other actions. Before the war started, many experts warned of what actually came to pass in Iraq: humanitarian disaster, political turmoil, new terrorist organizations, and distraction from unfinished business in Afghanistan. If President Bush had been willing to engage in compromise with his opposition while still holding firmly to his responsibility to protect America and root out terrorism, his administration might have achieved its objectives by avoiding the Iraq War altogether, laying better postwar plans, or building a stronger international coalition.

By contrast, the first President Bush used compromise—while asserting and preserving his values—on a number of occasions. In a 1999 address in the Old Senate Chamber, Bush Sr. reflected on his efforts to practice bipartisanship, consensus, and compromise during his administration. While thoroughly acknowledging the challenges of seeking compromise, he pointed to two legislative victories that resulted from it. In his words, "both the Clean Air Acts and the Americans with Disabilities Act were landmark pieces of legislation that became a reality only after the White House and the Senate demonstrated bipartisanship and compromise." Perhaps his best-known compromise involved working with a Democratic Congress to raise taxes in order to reduce serious budget deficits, even though doing so forced him to go back on the famous promise of "no new taxes" he made at the 1988 Republican National Convention.

Persuasion or Coercion?

In Chapter Three, we looked at the importance of using persuasion to advance our values in the public square. Persuasion refers to the practice of working to change others' hearts and minds by *convincing* them that our vision of the common good is the best way to achieve a healthy and productive society. The opposite of persuasion is *coercion*: using force, including military power and the power of the state, to compel others to live by our values, even against their own will. Persuasion is a positive action based on encouragement, rational argument, and debate.

To be sure, there are some times when coercion is necessary, as in the case of just wars and using force to defend ourselves against imminent threats. But when not used as an option of last resort, the effects of coercion can be disastrous—as evidenced by the Iraq War and numerous other armed conflicts around the globe. Other examples of coercion are much more mundane. Between 1920 and 1933, a constitutional amendment banned the sale and consumption of alcohol throughout the United States. Though Prohibition, as it is commonly called, had enough legislative backing to pass, it was generally unpopular and fueled the explosive growth of black market alcohol production and the rise of notorious gangsters like Al Capone. The amendment was such a failure that Congress and the states repealed it in 1933.

More recently, the No Child Left Behind Act attempted to coerce urban schools to perform better by penalizing them for failing to meet certain standards rather than rewarding schools that did well. And then there's the preponderance of "51 percent" strategies among political campaigns on both sides of the aisle, which seek just enough support to win elections and ensure that a tiny majority will hold sway over the entire constituency.

Wouldn't we be better off if our leaders worked to build real majorities that are capable of supporting and enacting the sorts of changes our nation so desperately needs?

How can we work to persuade others? When culture warriors began to set their sights on undocumented immigrants in recent years, calling for a coercive strategy of stricter penalties for those who enter the United States illegally and harsh action against employers who hire these immigrants, the United States Conference of Catholic Bishops countered with a persuasive campaign called Justice for Immigrants (http://www.justiceforimmigrants. org). Justice for Immigrants operates on the principle that our nation must enact immigration reform in ways that respect human dignity and keep families intact. In this respect, it works to help Catholics and other Americans understand the human dimension of immigration: that regardless of citizenship, all human beings have the same God-given rights and worth. This necessarily carries a policy component, which focuses not on building bigger walls and hiring more border guards but rather on addressing the economic forces—the root causes—that drive immigration. As the USCCB wrote in a 2003 joint letter with the bishops of Mexico titled *Strangers No Longer: Together on the Journey of Hope*, "The Church recognizes that all goods of the earth belong to all people. When persons cannot find employment in their country of origin to support themselves and their families, they have a right to find work elsewhere in order to survive. Sovereign nations should provide ways to accommodate this right." Using its moral authority, the Church is working to persuade Catholics and other Americans of the responsibility to share our prosperity with others.

Faith, Politics, and the Future of America

It seems likely that faith will remain a major feature in national politics for years to come. But the parameters of the "faith in public life" debate will probably always remain in a constant state of flux. In the wake of the bitter contentions of 2004, we witnessed firsthand—in the 2006 midterm elections and subsequent presidential campaigns—how candidates of both parties began to enunciate the role faith plays in their own personal lives. We also saw Americans of all faith traditions begin to pay more attention to the religious dimensions and the threats to human dignity of such issues as war, immigration, health care, poverty, and global climate change.

This is particularly the case in our Catholic community. From the Justice for Immigrants campaign to the Vatican's environmental work to the USCCB's 2007 *Faithful Citizenship* document, the Catholic message that people of all creeds and nationalities ought to look beyond partisan politics to a comprehensive vision of the common good is gaining widespread traction. This vision of the common good is one of our church's most important gifts to the world. It is an essential road map to overcoming the politics of division and building a nation for all.

In this era of globalization and technological revolution, however, American lay Catholics must embrace a more demanding role as our church faces a time of unprecedented change. As Joseph Bottum of the *Weekly Standard* magazine observed in 2006, "This may be the best time in American history to be a Catholic, and it may also be the worst: a moment of triumph after 200 years of outsiderness, and an occasion of mockery and shame. It is an era in which a surprisingly large portion of the nation's serious moral analysis seems to derive from Catholic sources." Indeed, even as some parishes are shrinking or changing under financial pressures resulting in part from scandals associated with priests' sexual abuse of young people, the political influence of individual Catholics continues to grow in the United States. With 25 U.S. senators and 130 congressional representatives, Catholics make up the largest single religious denomination in Congress. They hold a majority of seats on the U.S. Supreme Court and lead countless major corporations. And Catholic colleges and universities continue to rank among our nation's most respected institutions of higher education.

Georgetown University theologian Vincent Miller argues that the technological and media revolution is now influencing the Catholic faith in profound and unprecedented ways. For centuries, Catholics' relationships with the Church have been cultivated primarily at the local parish level. But starting in the 1990s, a "new ecclesial space" began to emerge, with secular TV and print news replacing traditional institutional structures as the predominant means by which everyday lay Catholics learn about Church matters. Like it or not, the pope, bishops, and parish priests are no longer the only vehicles by which the messages of the Church reach individual Catholics and the wider world. That distinction now falls to laypeople like Catholic League president Bill Donohue, a far right culture warrior whose grasp of modern communications strategies has allowed him to become a regular commentator on cable news programs—an "official" Catholic spokesperson, in the eyes of many—despite the fact that he has no authority to speak for the Church institution.

More recently, the Internet has emerged as a powerful new way to communicate Catholic teaching and theology and to dialogue with others as to how best to apply the values of our faith to public life. Younger Catholics in particular are beginning to organize using social networking sites like MySpace and Facebook, building organizations like Catholics United and ad hoc movements like Catholics for an End to the War in Iraq. Countless blogs and Internet message boards have sprung up to discuss contemporary Catholic issues—some of them garnering a regular audience of national readership—and news services like Catholic Online and Catholics in Alliance's *Catholic Media Report* are flourishing. The result is an unprecedented democratization of Catholic communications, as conversations once relegated to the ivory towers of the seminary are now carried out in very public ways. If Miller is correct, the future of the Church's ability to deliver its messages to the wider society and culture lies in part in the hands of those who will use this media most effectively. It's up to us to ensure that this power is not abused.

The media revolution our church community is now experiencing mirrors a transformation under way in our broader society, culture, and politics. With increasing amounts of cash flowing into hotly contested elections and the growing influence of conflict-hungry cable TV news channels, the effects of modern media—and its potential for misuse—grows stronger every day.

What do we make of all this? On the one hand, the modern media have created more transparency in our political system, allowing the public to hold its leaders, candidates, and officials accountable in unprecedented ways. At the same time, this unforgiving media culture provides the perfect sort of environment in which the politics of division can thrive. In the presidential primaries of 2008, for example, many Americans felt that the media helped foment personal attacks among the candidates and gave too little coverage to the important ideas and issues of the campaign.

It is for this reason that, as in our church community, we can't as citizens afford to stand on the sidelines as casual observers of what we might consider a great media or political game. Democracy is neither a spectator sport nor a reality show; its purpose is not to keep us pacified and entertained. Quite the contrary, it is a social and cultural endeavor that carries real and far-reaching consequences. Checking out of this process or letting it take its own course carries the likely danger that the biggest losers will be ourselves.

The culture warriors who preach the politics of division are still far ahead of the mainstream in getting their message to market, and as we have seen, the effects of this media muscle on our church and our political system have been devastating. In this moment, when sound-bite pundits speak more for their constituencies or their partisan agendas than for the common good, the fundamental challenge we face as people of faith and believers in justice is to keep the integrity of our own message alive. But the information revolution has provided a new opportunity to citizens and activists seeking to reclaim common good values from those who would prefer to see them swept under the proverbial rug. And at a time when the themes of hope, unity, and "working together" appear to be emerging as the defining political and social narratives of the twenty-first century, it appears that America may be poised to rise again as a nation that truly exists for all.

There has scarcely been a better opportunity for members of our church who are passionate about the common good to embrace their identity as Catholic Americans, and to help bring the light of our faith's message of justice and dignity to the farthest reaches of our nation and our world.

Resources on Catholic Social Teaching and the Common Good

Books

Barber, Benjamin R. *Consumed: How Markets Corrupt Children, Infantilize Adults, and Swallow Citizens Whole.* New York: Norton, 2007.

Cahill, Lisa Sowle. *Love Your Enemies: Discipleship, Pacifism, and Just War Theory.* Minneapolis, Minn.: Augsburg Fortress, 1994.

Catechism of the Catholic Church. New York: Bantam Doubleday, 1995.

Collins, Chuck, and Mary Wright. *The Moral Measure of the Economy.* Maryknoll, N.Y.: Orbis Books, 2007.

Deberri, Edward P., James E. Hug, Peter J. Henriot, and Michael J. Schulteis. *Catholic Social Teaching: Our Best Kept Secret.* Maryknoll, N.Y.: Orbis Books, 2003.

Dionne, E. J. *Why Americans Hate Politics.* New York, N.Y.: Simon & Schuster/Touchstone, 1991.

Glendon, Mary Ann. *Rights Talk: The Impoverishment of Political Discourse.* New York: Free Press, 1993.

Groody, Daniel G. *Globalization, Spirituality, and Justice.* Maryknoll, N.Y.: Orbis Books, 2007.

Groody, Daniel G. (ed.). *The Option for the Poor in Christian Theology.* Notre Dame, Ind.: University of Notre Dame Press, 2007.

Heyer, Kristin E. *Prophetic and Public: The Social Witness of U.S. Catholicism.* Washington, D.C.: Georgetown University Press, 2006.

Himes, Kenneth R. *Responses to 101 Questions on Catholic Social Teaching.* Mahwah, N.J.: Paulist Press, 2001.

Himes, Kenneth R., Lisa Sowell Cahill, Charles E. Curran, David Hollenbach, and Thomas A. Shannon (eds.). *Modern Catholic Social Teaching: Commentaries and Interpretations.* Washington, D.C.: Georgetown University Press, 2004.

Hogan, John P. *Credible Signs of Christ Alive: Case Studies from the Catholic Campaign for Human Development.* Lanham, Md.: Rowman & Littlefield, 2003.

Hollenbach, David. *The Common Good and Christian Ethics*. Cambridge: Cambridge University Press, 2002.

Hunter, James Davison. *Culture Wars: The Struggle to Define America*. New York: Basic Books, 1991.

Keys, Mary M. *Aquinas, Aristotle, and the Promise of the Common Good*. New York: Cambridge University Press, 2006.

Massaro, Thomas. *Living Justice: Catholic Social Teaching in Action*. Lanham, Md.: Rowman & Littlefield, 2000.

Massaro, Thomas, and Thomas A. Shannon (eds.). *American Catholic Social Teaching*. Collegeville, Minn.: Liturgical Press, 2002.

McGreevy, John T. *Catholicism and American Freedom: A History*. New York: Norton, 2003.

Miller, Vincent J. *Consuming Religion: Christian Faith and Practice in a Consumer Culture*. New York: Continuum, 2003.

Murray, John Courtney. *We Hold These Truths: Catholic Reflections on the American Proposition*. Lanham, Md.: Rowman & Littlefield, 2005.

Neuhaus, Richard John. *The Naked Public Square: Religion and Democracy in America* (2nd ed.). Grand Rapids, Mich.: Eerdmans, 1986.

O'Brien, David J. *Public Catholicism*. New York: Palgrave Macmillan, 1989.

O'Brien, David J., and Thomas A. Shannon (eds.). *Catholic Social Thought: The Documentary Heritage*. Maryknoll, N.Y.: Orbis Books, 1992.

Pontifical Council for Justice and Peace. *Compendium of the Social Doctrine of the Church*. Washington, D.C.: United States Conference of Catholic Bishops, 2005.

Putnam, Robert D. *Bowling Alone: The Collapse and Revival of American Community*. New York: Simon & Schuster, 2000.

Reese, Thomas J. *A Flock of Shepherds: The National Conference of Catholic Bishops*. Kansas City, Mo.: Sheed & Ward, 1992.

Wallis, Jim. *God's Politics: Why the Right Gets It Wrong and the Left Doesn't Get It*. New York: HarperCollins, 2005.

Weigel, George, and Robert Royal (eds.). *Building the Free Society: Democracy, Capitalism, and Catholic Social Teaching*. Grand Rapid, Mich.: Eerdmans, 1993.

Weigert, Kathleen Mass, and Alexia K. Kelley. *Living the Catholic Social Tradition: Cases and Commentary*. Lanham, Md.: Rowman & Littlefield, 2004.

Wolfe, Alan. *One Nation, After All: What Americans Really Think About God, Country, Family, Racism, Welfare, Immigration, Homosexuality, Work, the Right, the Left, and Each Other*. New York: Penguin Books, 1998.

Papal Encyclicals and Other Church Documents

Congregation for the Doctrine of the Faith, *Doctrinal Note on Some Questions Regarding the Participation of Catholics in Political Life*, November 24, 2002.

Pope Benedict XVI, *Deus Caritas Est* (God Is Love), December 25, 2005.

Pope Benedict XVI, *Spe Salvi* (Saved by Hope), November 30, 2007.

Pope John XXIII, *Mater et Magistra* (Christianity and Social Progress), May 15, 1961.

Pope John XXIII, *Pacem in Terris* (Peace on Earth), April 11, 1963.

Pope John Paul II, *Evangelium Vitae* (The Gospel of Life), March 15, 1995.

Pope John Paul II, *Laborem Exercens* (On Human Work), September 14, 1981.

Pope John Paul II, *Sollicitudo Rei Socialis* (On Social Concern), December 30, 1987.

Pope John Paul II, *Centesimus Annus* (On the Hundredth Anniversary), May 1, 1991.

Pope Leo XIII, *Rerum Novarum* (Of New Things), May 15, 1891.

Pope Paul VI, *Octogesima Adveniens* (A Call to Action), May 14, 1971.

Pope Paul VI, *Populorum Progressio* (The Development of Peoples), March 26, 1967.

Pope Pius XI, *Quadragesimo Anno* (In the Fortieth Year), May 15, 1931.

Second Vatican Council, *Dignitatis Humanae* (Declaration on Religious Freedom), December 7, 1965.

Second Vatican Council, *Gaudium et Spes* (The Pastoral Constitution on the Church in the Modern World), December 8, 1965.

United States Conference of Catholic Bishops, *The Challenge of Peace*, May 3, 1983.

United States Conference of Catholic Bishops, *A Decade After* Economic Justice for All: *Continuing Principles, Changing Context, New Challenges*, November 1995.

United States Conference of Catholic Bishops, *Economic Justice for All: Pastoral Letter on Catholic Social Teaching and the U.S. Economy*, 1986.

United States Conference of Catholic Bishops, *Faithful Citizenship: A Catholic Call to Political Responsibility*, November 2003.

United States Conference of Catholic Bishops, *Forming Consciences for Faithful Citizenship: A Call to Political Responsibility from the Bishops of the United States*, November 14, 2007.

United States Conference of Catholic Bishops and Conferencia del Episcopado Mexicano, *Strangers No Longer: Together on the Journey of Hope*, January 22, 2003.

Other Organizations

ACORN—http://www.acorn.org

> ACORN, the Association of Community Organizations for Reform Now, is the nation's largest organization of low- and moderate-income families, working together for social justice and stronger communities. ACORN's accomplishments include successful campaigns for better housing, schools, neighborhood safety, health care, job conditions, and more.

Association of Catholic Colleges and Universities (ACCU)—http://www.accunet.org

> Founded in 1899, ACCU is the collective voice of Catholic higher education in the United States. Through seminars, conferences, publications, research, and consultation, ACCU helps foster a vibrant Catholic identity at member institutions and supports cooperation among them for the greater good of society and the Church.

Association of Jesuit Colleges and Universities (AJCU)—http://www.ajcunet.edu/

> AJCU supports and promotes U.S. Jesuit higher education by facilitating cooperative efforts among and providing services to its twenty-eight member institutions, providing a forum for the exchange of experience and information, and representing the work of U.S. Jesuit higher education at the national and international levels.

Bread for the World—http://www.bread.org

> Bread for the World is a nationwide Christian movement that seeks justice for the world's hungry people by lobbying our nation's decision makers.

Busted Halo—http://www.bustedhalo.com

> Busted Halo is an online magazine for spiritual speakers in their twenties and thirties run by the Paulist Fathers.

Catholic Campaign for Human Development (CCHD)—http://www.usccb.org/cchd

> CCHD is the domestic antipoverty and social justice program of the United States Conference of Catholic Bishops. Its mission is to address the root causes of poverty in America through promotion and support of community-controlled self-help organizations and through transformative education.

Catholic Charities USA—http://www.catholiccharitiesusa.org

> Catholic Charities USA serves as the national voice for the Catholic Charities network and the people it helps by vigorously advocating

federal policymakers on our poverty reduction agenda and promoting the work of local Catholic Charities and federal legislative agenda to the media and the general public.

Catholic Health Association (CHA)—http://www.chausa.org

CHA is the nation's largest group of not-for-profit health care sponsors, systems, and facilities. It works to serve the nation's Catholic health care organizations and support the strategic directions of mission, ethics, and advocacy.

Catholic Legal Immigration Network, Inc. (CLINIC)—http://www.clinic legal.org

CLINIC works to enhance and expand delivery of legal services to indigent and low-income immigrants principally through diocesan immigration programs and to meet the immigration needs identified by the Catholic Church in the United States.

Catholic Relief Services (CRS)—http://www.crs.org

CRS is the official international relief and development agency of the U.S. Catholic community. It serves the poor in over one hundred countries overseas through programs in emergency relief, HIV/AIDS, health, agriculture, education, microfinance, and peace-building.

Catholics Against Capital Punishment (CACP)—http://www.cacp.org

CACP strives to ensure that members of the clergy and laypeople—both Catholic and non-Catholic—are aware of and understand the seriousness of Church teachings on capital punishment. It seeks to instill in elected officials the courage to resist the temptation to support the death penalty as a politically expedient way of promoting themselves as "tough on crime."

Catholics in Alliance for the Common Good—http://www.catholicsin alliance.org

Catholics in Alliance for the Common Good is a nonpartisan, nonprofit 501(c)(3) organization dedicated to promoting the fullness of the Catholic social tradition in the public square. Founded in 2005, its mission is to provide information to Catholics about Church social teaching as it relates to public participation in our society and to advance the prophetic voice of the Catholic social tradition.

Catholics United—http://www.catholics-united.org

Catholics United is a nonprofit, nonpartisan 501(c)(4) organization dedicated to promoting the message of justice and the common good found at the heart of the Catholic social tradition. It accomplishes this mission through online advocacy and educational activities.

Center of Concern—http://www.coc.org

The Center of Concern works to provide individuals and organizations with basic tools to address the root causes of human suffering in the world today and explore ways to change the system to increase social justice and offer hope. It provides reliable information and analysis on development issues, practical alternatives to current development policies, practical suggestions for personal action, and faith reflections on this work for justice.

Christian Churches Together (CCT)—http://www.christianchurchestogeth er.org

CCT is a new forum growing out of a deeply felt need to broaden and expand fellowship, unity, and witness among the diverse expressions of Christian faith today. It provides a context—marked by prayer, theological dialogue, and fellowship—in which churches can develop relationships with other churches with whom they presently have little contact.

Christian Life Communities(CLC)—http://www.clc-usa.org

The mission of the CLC is to enable the widespread sharing and authentic living of our vision in the Church and culture of the United States of America. It seeks to provide interested and affiliated communities with resources that flow out of our vision.

Conference of Major Superiors of Men (CMSM)—http://www.cmsm.org

CMSM serves the leadership of the Catholic orders and congregations of the more than twenty thousand vowed religious priests and brothers of the United States, 10 percent of whom are foreign missionaries. CMSM provides a voice for these communities in the U.S. Church and society. CMSM also collaborates with the USCCB and other key groups and organizations that serve church and society.

Faith in Public Life—http://www.faithinpubliclife.org

Faith in Public Life strengthens the effectiveness, collaboration, and reach of faith movements that share a call to pursue justice and the common good. A 501(c)(3) organization, it provides organizing and communications resources to diverse faith leaders and organizations.

Franciscan Mission Service—http://franciscanmissionservice.org

Franciscan Mission Service prepares and places Catholic laypersons in international Franciscan mission sites staffed or supervised by

Franciscan laity and religious. Missioners serve a three-year commitment, renewable once, whereupon they return to the United States and continue to live out their call to mission as reverse missioners.

Gamaliel Foundation—http://www.gamaliel.org

The Gamaliel Foundation works to assist local community leaders to create, maintain, and expand independent, grassroots, and powerful faith-based community organizations so that ordinary people can influence the political, social, economic, and environmental decisions that affect their lives; to provide these organizations with leadership training programs, consultation, research, and analysis on social justice issues; and to be a network for mutual learning environments and working coalitions.

Ignatian Solidarity Network (ISN)—http://www.ignatiansolidarity.net

ISN works to facilitate and enhance the effectiveness of existing social justice and advocacy efforts that are currently present in Jesuit-affiliated high schools, universities and colleges, parishes, retreat centers, and independent organizations and among lay individuals across the nation. The network serves as a means to connect, strengthen, and broaden communication among these already existing groups in order to better understand what it means to live and act upon "a faith that does justice."

Institute for Black Catholic Studies (IBCS)—http://www.xula.edu/IBCS

IBCS assists black and cross-cultural priests, religious, laypersons, seminarians, novices, catechists, diocesan administrators, deacons, lay associates, and volunteers from African American and other cultural heritages who are engaged in ministry among black Catholics and the broader pan-African community in the United States. Its goal is to help students develop more meaningful and culturally effective ministerial strategies for the evangelizing and social justice ministries of the Church within the culturally diverse black community.

Jesuit Volunteer Corps (JVC)—http://www.jesuitvolunteers.org

Since 1956, more than twelve thousand women and men have made a commitment to serve where the need is greatest through the Jesuit Volunteer Corps and found themselves "ruined for life." Jesuit Volunteers commit themselves to working with people who are marginalized by society and to living in apostolic community with other JVs.

JustFaith Ministries—http://www.justfaith.org

JustFaith Ministries strives to provide faith formation processes and resources that emphasize the gospel message of peace and justice,

Catholic social teaching, and the intersection of spirituality and action.

Knights of Malta—http://www.smom.org

The Order of Malta remains true to its inspiring principles, summarized in the motto "*Tuitio Fidei et Obsequium Pauperum*"—defense of the Faith and assistance to the poor and the suffering, which become reality through the voluntary work carried out by Dames and Knights in humanitarian assistance and medical and social activities.

Lane Center for Catholic Studies and Social Thought—http://www.usfca .edu/lanecenter

The Joan and Ralph Lane Center for Catholic Studies and Social Thought at the University of San Francisco (USF) enriches and enlivens the Jesuit, Catholic character of USF and engages and develops Catholic social thought for the Church, the city, and the world. The Center advances the scholarship and application of the Catholic intellectual tradition in the Church and society with an emphasis on social concerns.

Leadership Conference of Women Religious (LCWR)—http://www.lcwr.org

LCWR is the association of the leaders of congregations of Catholic women religious in the United States. Founded in 1956, the conference helps its members collaboratively carry out their service of leadership to further the mission of the gospel in today's world.

Maryknoll Office for Global Concerns—http://www.maryknollogc.org

The Office for Global Concerns serves Maryknoll missioners by providing analysis and advocacy on justice and peace issues that affect the communities where Maryknollers live and work. Maryknoll missioners work in some forty countries around the world, emphasizing global solidarity and the transformation of systems and structures that perpetuate injustice, oppression, and environmental destruction, as well as the identification of those that promote human dignity and ecological well-being.

National Advocacy Center of the Sisters of the Good Shepherd—http://www. gsadvocacy.org

Through contemplation and action, their mission of reconciliation impels the Sisters of the Good Shepherd to act with justice and peace. The Sisters minister in all areas of human services, with a particular focus on the needs of women and children.

National Black Catholic Congress—http://www.nbccongress.org

> The National Black Catholic Congress, made up of member organizations, represents African American Roman Catholics, working in collaboration with National Roman Catholic organizations. The Congress is committed to establishing an agenda for the evangelization of African Americans and to improving the spiritual, mental, and physical conditions of African Americans.

National Catholic Council of Hispanic Ministries (NCCHM)—http://www.ncchm.com

> NCCHM was formed in 1991 to create broadly based networks to share mutual concerns with its member organizations. Given the diversity of the United States Hispanic Catholic communities, such an umbrella organization is essential if the problems and possibilities of these groups are to be articulated and communicated effectively in the Church and in the broader society.

National Catholic Rural Life Conference (NCRLC)—http://www.ncrlc.com

> NCRLC provides spiritual, educational, and advocacy assistance to help rural people shape their own destinies and lead lives of dignity.

National Pastoral Life Center—http://www.nplc.org

> The National Pastoral Life Center serves the leadership of the church's pastoral ministry, particularly in parishes and diocesan offices. Founded in 1983 by Reverend Monsignor Philip J. Murnion with the encouragement of the National Conference of Catholic Bishops, the center assembles the best of thinking and practice—through its studies, publications, consulting, and conferences—contributing to reflective and effective pastoral ministry.

NETWORK, a National Catholic Social Justice Lobby—http://www.networklobby.org

> NETWORK is a progressive voice within the Catholic community that has been influencing Congress in favor of peace and justice for more than thirty years. Through lobbying and legislative advocacy, it strives to close the gap between rich and poor and to dismantle policies rooted in racism, greed, and violence. NETWORK's membership, which includes both individuals and organizations, represents more than one hundred thousand people.

Oblates of Saint Francis DeSales—http://www.oblates.org

> The Oblates of Saint Francis DeSales are a religious order of men. The Oblates believe in the dignity, worth, and responsible liberty of each person, and they try to approach each person in a gentle and humble way while fostering peace and justice in the world community.

ONE Campaign—http://www.one.org

> ONE is Americans of all beliefs and every walk of life—united as ONE—to help make poverty history. ONE is raising public awareness about the issues of global poverty, hunger, disease, and efforts to fight such problems in the world's poorest countries.

Organization for Economic Cooperation and Development (OECD)—http://www.oecd.org

> The OECD brings together the governments of countries committed to democracy and the market economy from around the world to support sustainable economic growth, boost employment, raise living standards, maintain financial stability, assist other countries' economic development, and contribute to growth in world trade.

Pax Christi USA—http://www.paxchristiusa.org

> Pax Christi USA strives to create a world that reflects the Peace of Christ by exploring, articulating, and witnessing to the call of Christian nonviolence. Pax Christi USA rejects war, preparations for war, and every form of violence and domination. It advocates primacy of conscience, economic and social justice, and respect for Creation.

PICO—http://www.piconetwork.org

> PICO builds community organizations based on religious congregations, schools, and community centers, which are often the only stable civic gathering places in many neighborhoods. As a result, PICO federations are able to engage thousands of people and sustain long-term campaigns to bring about systematic change at all levels of government.

SC Ministry Foundation—http://www.scministryfdn.org

> The SC Ministry Foundation of the Sisters of Charity of Cincinnati supports organizations that further social justice by addressing root causes of poverty, racism, and oppression.

Sisters of Mercy of the Americas—http://www.sistersofmercy.org

> The Sisters of Mercy are an international community of women religious vowed to serve people who suffer from poverty, sickness, and lack of education with a special concern for women and children.

Sojourners—http://www.sojo.net

> Sojourners works to articulate the biblical call to social justice, inspiring hope and building a movement to transform individuals, communities, the church, and the world.

Tekakwitha Conference—http://groups.creighton.edu/tekconf

> The Tekakwitha Conference strives to unify the Native American Catholic voice, presence, and identity while respecting diversity. It further strives to empower Native American Catholics in the Church and to deepen and affirm Native American Catholics' identity and pride in their culture and spiritual traditions.

U.S. Catholic Mission Association (USCMA)—http://www.uscatholicmission.org

> USCMA unites and supports people committed to the cross-cultural and global mission of Jesus Christ in service to Church and the world.

United for a Fair Economy (UFE)—http://www.faireconomy.org

> UFE is a national, independent, nonpartisan 501(c)(3) nonprofit organization. It raises awareness that concentrated wealth and power undermine the economy, corrupt democracy, deepen the racial divide, and tear communities apart.

United States Conference of Catholic Bishops—http://www.usccb.org

> The USCCB supports the ministry of bishops with an emphasis on evangelization, by which the bishops exercise in a communal and collegial manner certain pastoral functions entrusted to them by the Lord Jesus of sanctifying, teaching, and governing.

Woodstock Theological Center—http://woodstock.georgetown.edu

> The Woodstock Theological Center is an independent nonprofit institute at Georgetown University that engages in theological and ethical reflection on topics of social, economic, business, scientific, cultural, religious, and political importance. The center does research, conducts conferences and seminars, and publishes books and articles.

Election Day Checklist

Deciding how to vote can be difficult, but it is a task we all must take seriously and prayerfully in order to be faithful citizens. Our Church's social tradition calls us to consider a broad range of important issues—on everything from poverty to war, abortion, human rights, and the environment.

Because there is no Catholic voting formula, and rarely, if ever, a perfect candidate for Catholic voters, we must be prepared to use our prudential judgment, and make faithful and practical decisions at the voting booth. This checklist can help you make sound and informed choices on election day.

Inform Your Conscience

❑ Inform your conscience on the Church's social teachings by reading documents such as the U.S. Bishops' *Forming Consciences for Faithful Citizenship* (www.faithfulcitizenship .org), and by talking with your pastor.

❑ Research statements and voting records of the candidates on all the issues important to Catholics.

❑ Discuss matters of Catholic citizenship with family, friends, and leaders in your parish.

Apply Prudence to Choices

❏ Look for the candidate who will do the most in concrete terms to promote the dignity of human life, justice, and peace.

❏ Reject "Litmus Tests" that reduce Catholic issues to one or a few issues.

❏ Voting for a candidate who fails to endorse all of Church teaching can be justifiable if the candidate would produce results consistent with Church principles once in office.

Vote for the Common Good

❏ Will the candidate promote a society in which neighbors see each other as brothers and sisters? Will the candidate reject a get-what-you-can culture that validates greed and materialism?

❏ What will the candidate do to address affronts to human life and dignity—and their root causes—such as poverty, war, abortion, torture, the death penalty, and a lack of freedom and opportunity?

❏ Does the candidate believe that the health, security, and prosperity of our nation are linked to the health, security, and prosperity of the rest of the world? In short, does he or she believe we are in this together or going it alone?

❏ Does the candidate support an economic system that demands opportunity and human dignity for all—a living wage, health care, affordable education, and human rights?

❏ Does the candidate put principles ahead of power and personal profits? Does he or she respect the sacred trust between citizens and their public officials to put the common good ahead of special interests?

The Authors

Chris Korzen is cofounder and executive director of Catholics United, a nonpartisan online advocacy group dedicated to promoting social justice and the common good in U.S. public policy. Chris directed the Catholic Voting Project in 2004 and 2005 after working as a union organizer and software designer and as a volunteer activist with the Catholic social justice organization Pax Christi USA. He holds a master of theological studies degree from Weston Jesuit School of Theology in Cambridge, Massachusetts, and is a graduate of the College of the Holy Cross in Worcester, Massachusetts, and the Salt Institute for Documentary Studies in Portland, Maine.

Alexia Kelley is cofounder and executive director of Catholics in Alliance for the Common Good, a nonpartisan organization that promotes awareness of Catholic social teaching in the public square and supports the U.S. Catholic social justice movement. She has served in diverse capacities with nongovernmental organizations committed to poverty reduction, social justice, and the environment. Alexia worked for almost a decade at the Catholic Campaign for Human Development, the U.S. Catholic Bishops' national antipoverty program. She is coeditor of a book on Catholic social teaching, *Living the Catholic Social Tradition: Cases and Commentary*. Alexia holds a bachelor of arts degree in religion with honors from Haverford College and a master of theological studies degree in Christianity and Culture from Harvard Divinity School.

Index